The Digital Home Seller & Online Real Estate Trends
Industry Insider Secrets That Can Help You Save Thousands When Selling Your Own Home

By
Eric Eckardt

TABLE OF CONTENTS

PREFACE 4
MAKING THE DIGITAL HOME SELLER DECISION 19
THE INDUSTRY LANDSCAPE – DESIGNED FOR THE DIGITAL
HOME SELLER 28
LIST PRICE – METHODS & CONSIDERATIONS 43
PREPARING YOUR HOME FOR SALE 49
VIRTUAL HOME STAGING & SYNDICATION 56
THE BEST MOUSE TRAP – WHICH MODEL? 65
WORKING WITH LICENSED AGENTS 78
THE ART OF NEGOTIATING OFFERS 81
NAVIGATING THE CLOSING PROCESS 87
DEMYSTIFYING INDUSTRY MYTHS – CREATED BY REAL
ESTATE AGENTS 92
THE TRUTH ABOUT RESIDENTIAL REAL ESTATE – WHAT THE
INDUSTRY DOESN'T WANT YOU TO KNOW 97
WHY YOU WILL SUCCEED AS A DIGITAL HOME SELLER 108
THE FUTURE OF ONLINE REAL ESTATE 112
JOIN THE MOVEMENT 126

Appendix

Library of Congress Cataloging-in-Publication Data
Eckardt, Eric
The Digital Home Seller & Online Real Estate Trends / Eric Eckardt 1st ed.
1. Real estate 2. Digital trends 3. Home selling I. Title

Copyright © 2016 by Eric Eckardt
All rights reserved. No part of this book may be reproduced, scanned,
or distributed in any printed or electronic form without permission.
First Edition: July 2016
ISBN: 978-0-692-75440-5
Printed in the United States of America

PREFACE

I'd like to thank my family, friends and the many industry participants who were supportive of me embarking on this journey to publish the first (and long-overdue) guide to digital (self-direct) home selling. This book provides the most current and relevant material to enable anyone to sell their own home. What it does not include is any misguided information and it won't point you to resources and outdated methods from the 1990s (think handbooks and FSBO kits) that amazingly continue to still be used today. As an industry veteran, I believe that homeowners should be empowered to sell their own homes successfully and independently, and should be able to preserve their equity in the process. Using the proven techniques and methods in this book, independent home sellers will be able to leverage the newest online consumer trends and digital resources to maximize the digital home seller process. The **digital home seller movement** is spreading across the U.S. with a mission to eliminate the **$60 billion** in inflated, unnecessary commission fees that the real estate brokerage industry takes in from consumers on an annual basis. There has never been a better time to sell your own home, and this book will guide you on how to do so in the most efficient and effective way possible.

INTRODUCTION

I'll never forget, in was January 2004 I was working in investment banking in Manhattan. I thought it would be a good idea to get my real estate broker's license, given my previous success buying and selling investment properties. I was able to carve out time to satisfy the modest requirements, pass the state exams, and ultimately receive a waiver from the NYS Department of Licensing to become a broker overnight. During one of real estate licensing classes, I recall looking around at my classmates (50+ students) from various backgrounds, most of whom had zero direct experience in the industry or any professional training whatsoever. We were all planning on taking the real estate licensing salesperson exam. While I was shocked by how easy it was to get a license to legally advise people on buying and selling a home — something that can be one of the most important decisions in someone's life, I also recognized that there was a significant opportunity for me to launch my own independent real estate and mortgage company. A few months later, I exited investment banking, despite being told by almost everyone I knew that I was crazy to leave a great career on Wall Street; one where I was involved in originating over $10 billion in senior bank financing for Fortune 500 and middle-market companies. I recall my father, who was an active real estate investor, not speaking with me for several weeks after learning of my decision, given his past frustration with and perception of real estate agents. He thought I was taking my education, training and professional experience and throwing it out the window to join an industry where anyone — even someone like our seventy-year-old neighbor, who had no business acumen whatsoever — could become an agent was an agent.

I weathered through the storm of advice from close friends and family, and in 2004, I officially entered the real estate industry. I left Manhattan to launch two companies: a real estate company and a mortgage company in New York's Capital Region. I simultaneously sold both businesses simultaneously five years later, and in the years that followed I founded more companies in the real estate industry. In 2012, my company was nominated by one of the most prominent real estate publications in the industry, *Inman News*, as one of the most innovative online real estate startups. That same year, I exited that model after filing a direct public offering with the Securities Exchange Commission (SEC). I became a lead executive at one of the largest real estate brokerage firms in the U.S., and moved to Luxembourg to help lead its online real estate platforms. In 2015, I left this role and returned back home to the U.S. to launch another new real estate company, DwellOwner.com, a digital marketplace for home sellers and buyers.

While in Luxembourg, one of the online real estate platforms I led sold roughly 30,000 single family residential homes annually in the U.S. These were primarily distressed assets — bank foreclosures or short sales (a home that is sold for less than the amount owed on the mortgage, hence the term "short-sale.") These properties had mostly been taken over by a bank due to foreclosure or short sale, forcing families out of their homes for defaulting on their mortgage. Some of these borrowers had tried to sell their homes through a traditional agent prior to foreclosure, and were ultimately unsuccessful due in part to the 5 -7% agent commission mandated by real estate brokerages. There is over $60 billion in equity is stripped away from families on an annual basis by the real estate brokerage industry — and this practice has not changed in decades — despite online consumer trends, the advances of technology and broader market forces. The industry has been resistant to change and the establishment — led by the National Association of Realtors, franchises and larger independent brokerages — artificially inflating commission levels through the current multiple listing service (MLS) infrastructure and not necessarily competing on price.

I continue to be amazed when I see the same traditional real estate methods being employed: real estate signs that include agent headshots, advertisements for open houses constant (and pricey) solicitation materials being sent in the form of postcards, magnets, calendars and more from "local real estate experts." Over the past decade, not a lot has changed in the real estate brokerage industry, including inflated commissions and agent solicitation. It's all read off the same script. The requirements for real estate agents entering the field remain low as when I was first entering industry. There are over two million agents in the U.S. alone and amazingly, there is fierce competition between brokerages that have low accountability and enforce minimum professional standards, regardless of the real estate brand. Even slapping the name of a fancy conglomerate on a brokerage post company-acquisition doesn't really change things a whole lot. This, combined with the advent of online "marketplaces" like Zillow and Realtor.com has created a funnel that drives consumers directly to real estate agents whether they are buying or selling a home; making it seem as if there is no alternative. But there is an alternative, which is what motivated me to write this book. I have been on both sides of the industry for a number of years, and I have found that **today, there are VERY few reasons why any homeowner should use a traditional licensed real estate agent to sell their home at 5–7% commission,** and thereby strip away their equity. Online consumer trends, unprecedented access to a wealth of information and the number of options in the marketplace to self-manage a successful sale at a fraction of the cost are all reasons to support this claim.

In this book, I'll demystify a number of dated claims made over the past few decades by real estate agents who try to discourage homeowners from selling without an agent. We will delve into how homeowners can be empowered to successfully sell their home without a traditional real estate firm. This is outside of diving into online real estate trends and the market outlook for online real estate to empower home sellers.

Real Estate Commission Income

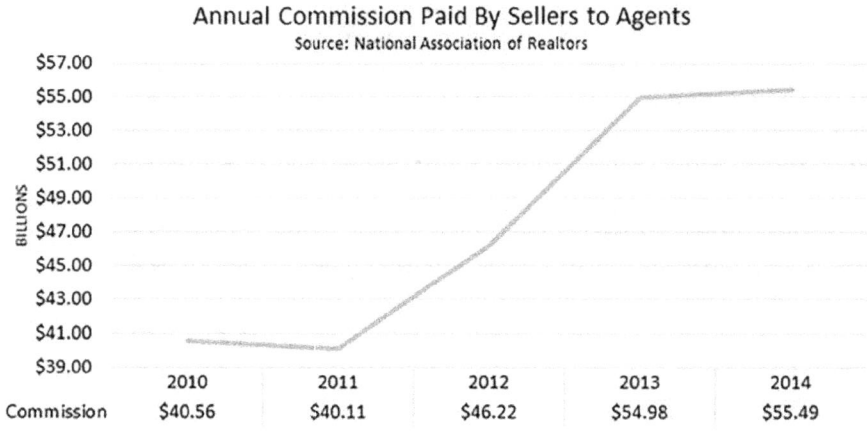

Source: NAR. In 2015, annual commission exceeded $60 billion

One of the few areas of innovation within the real estate industry is home discovery. Nearly 100% of homebuyers go online to search for a home on sites such as Zillow, Realtor.com, and Trulia (owned by Zillow). Outside of searching for a home and streamlining some of the processes, an archaic infrastructure still exists today, which benefits the multiple listing services (MLS) and licensed real estate agents and brokerages. In fact, the surge in Realtors is growing again, driven by the National Association of Realtors (NAR), despite the advancements in technology and changes in consumer behavior. Real estate is one of the few industries that technology hasn't impacted or disrupted, unlike other industries such as retail stock trading, travel and retail goods and services. The number of retail stockbrokers and travel agents has declined significantly since the advent of the internet, forcing the redefinition of these jobs and in turn driving efficiency and cost savings for the consumer. In contrast the real estate industry has resisted and has in fact done everything in its power to prevent a reformation. As a result, commission rates have remained unchanged, stripping billions in equity from homeowners from on an annual basis. We cite several examples in this book with the National Association of Realtors (NAR) and reference several organizations, including the Consumer Protection Bureau and U.S. Department of Justice, that have targeted the real estate brokerage industry to influence change.

NAR currently controls over 1,200 separate local Realtor associations that dictate business practices and encourage membership across the industry. If a broker joins a local association the bylaws typically require that every agent in their office join so that dues can be captured and funneled to the head of the Real Estate Cartel, which is the National Association of Realtors.

NAR Licensed Real Estate Agent Members[1]
2016 = 1,187,786
2015 = 1,167,595
2014 = 1,099,102
2013 = 1,042,231
2012 =   999,824
2011 = 1,009,940
2010 = 1,066,658

In 2015, the National Association of Realtors' "DANGER" report (Definitive Analysis of Negative Game Changers Emerging in Real Estate) acknowledged that consumers were demanding lower commission rates and that brokers and agents were responding with new pricing models that **"will most likely become commonplace in the next 5 to 10 years."**[2] International buyers are particularly shocked by the high commissions paid in the United States, as the average commission paid to realty agents in places such as the United Kingdom, Australia and Belgium ranges from 1-3% versus the 5-7% rate which is common in the U.S. Usually, high commission fees are found in less developed countries with no public records and no reliable MLS. For example, in Belarus, commission rates can range from 5-15% but in other countries such as China and Greece, the government imposes high transfer taxes at 15% that discourage the transfer of property.

This is, of course, not the case in the U.S. Here we have a more efficient infrastructure, well documented public records and ease of transferability, and yet the real estate commission rates here are still one of the highest in the world among developed nations.

Select Global Real Estate Brokerage Fees[3]

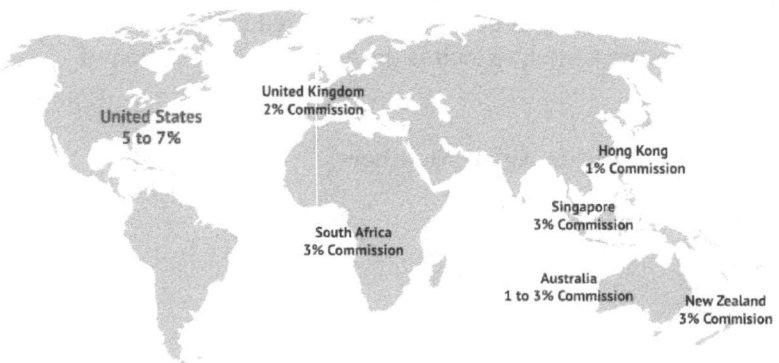

For decades, real estate commission fees have been viewed as grossly inefficient and much debate has centered on the expectation that they would trend lower. It has been quite the opposite in the U.S. with organizations like the NAR and large corporate franchise entities controlling the model. The U.S. was expecting an increase in efficiency that would lead to lower commission rates, but economists and other researchers had not factored in the resistance the NAR and other organizations.

The good news is, that despite the resistance from the industry, it has never been easier to sell your own home as an informed home seller, thus saving thousands of dollars in unnecessary inflated commission fees — that have charged by real estate agents for decades. Nearly 100% of homebuyers search online to find homes and they generally start looking six months in advance of contacting an agent. Some of the FSBO platforms in the market today offer the ability to choose from various service offerings depending on need. The market remains highly fragmented and unfortunately, if you Google "FSBO," you'll see many FSBO business models promoting business practices from the 1990s, capturing fees upfront and suggesting antiquated methods to sell your home. I explore these "FSBO" models in Chapter 6, and provide guidance on what to look for and what to avoid when choosing a service that will provide access to the MLS. Not surprisingly, all business models are not created equal.

> Unfortunately, there are still home seller books in circulation that discuss open houses and classified ads in local newspapers, where to place the yard sign and other outdated methods to sell homes that are being advocated to private home sellers. Some have been released within the last two years.

The Problem with home seller (FSBO) Books, Websites, Online Videos and Other Sources

Many of the real-estate-for-home-seller guides and general offerings (which are sometimes referred to as self-direct seller, for-sale-by-owner resources) feature antiquated content and business practices that aren't aligned with the online consumer — even some of the more recent guides that have been released over the past few years! I still see material out there talking about conducting open houses (of which less than 9% results in a sale) and preparing display advertisements in local newspapers (ignoring nearly all buyers search online). There are even business models selling flier boxes and other archaic items to prospective home sellers online while trying to upsell them on advisory services, along with third-party, generic state forms. It's concerning to see how many models exist, many of which are not aligned with the current market dynamics and do not offering the best solution to sell your own home. This is especially true of the current market, which is highly fragmented with a changing landscape driven by consumer behavior. There are even new participants, backed by public and private equity entities, that are trying to cash in on the $60 billion commission real estate. Most lack the right leadership and/or the ability to truly understand market dynamics to successfully bring to market a viable consumer offering.

I have observed significant changes in the market, even recently, with new technologies such as artificial intelligence, blockchain technology and virtual reality. These items can influence new processes, enhancing consumer experience and business methods while putting pressure on the traditional real estate brokerage model and providing salvation to the millions of people who try to sell their home each year.

Empowering the Average Homeowner

I created *Digital Home Seller & Online Real Estate Trends* because the plethora of misinformation that prevails throughout the real estate industry, the NAR cartel and the advent of real estate technology made me recognize that a publication such as this, one that empowers consumers with best practices that really work, was long overdue. This book takes you through the whole process, from the decision to sell a home to how to get it done yourself. (Sadly, there are many homes today that are listed with nothing more than unprofessional still photos and limited market data, which prevents the prospective home buyers who are searching online from making informed decisions.) You'll learn about online staging optimization using 3D virtual tours, how to host a 24/7 open house and more, all from your mobile device. I'll even walk you through the different methodologies on pricing and explain how to arrive at current market values. (In Chapter 5 we provide guidance on preparing your home sale. I don't elaborate on cleaning and moving furniture around; I just highlight what's important.) I also provide an overview of the current market landscape, and I support my concepts with statistical facts, real-life market and financial industry experience and other data, all of which illustrate why you should be selling your own home independently. I then define what's most imperative when putting your home on the market (with regard to pricing and online positioning) and provide you with the best practices and tactics that will allow you to achieve great success in maximizing your financial exposure.

Importantly, this book will also give you a sense of the profile of a typical homebuyer by examining online real estate trends, market behavior and will share ways to position your home in order to gain the most market exposure. I do this by leveraging all mediums through a multi-channel approach, going beyond what a typical real estate agent would offer. I'll also relay forecasted growth across different demographics, including the robust Gen X and Millennial markets, and how their behavior influences the market.

In Chapter 11, I share an insider perspective on the industry and sum up how you can use it to navigate the market landscape to successfully sell your own home without a traditional, licensed real estate agent. This section includes an overview of prevailing market misconceptions and what the industry doesn't want you know—I couldn't resist! I also report on the new hybrid, online real estate models that have recently become available.

The real estate industry is changing and I am proud to be part of the digital home seller movement, empowering homeowners while allowing families to preserve their hard-earned equity. My last chapter delves into the future of online real estate; this is topic that I am quite passionate about as it has the potential to influence long overdue change in the industry, making it better for the consumer. It's also changing as I write this as advances in technology have brought us artificial intelligence (AI), virtual reality, blockchain technology and identify potential new retail participants. These are all topics that are covered in Chapter 13 and are very exciting as they are driving immediate efficiencies vertically integrate in the brokerage space.

Digital Home Seller & Online Real Estate Trends was indeed written to empower home sellers to save thousands in commission expenses teaching them how to avoid falling victim to paying exorbitant sell-side commissions. However, it was also written to inspire broader industry participants: venture capital investors, licensed real estate agents and brokers, basically anyone who wants to understand the current market dynamics for online real estate. Real estate agents can use this information to reevaluate their value proposition to stay relevant while brokers can adapt their business models to align with consumer trends. Investors can learn about the current landscape and potential new segments for growth within our space to deploy investment capital.

> Join the movement to accelerate change in the real estate industry! After finishing this book, you can continue to stay informed about the industry by visiting DwellOwner.com, which features an intelligent, interactive community of like-minded real estate activists, industry professionals, and offers downloadable forms, home seller videos, and reports on best practices.

1
MAKING THE DIGITAL HOME SELLER DECISION

"Today, there really no reason why anyone should be paying the traditional 5-7% real estate commission rate to sell their own home."

Given the current trends in the marketplace — specifically the advent of the "online buyer" — there has never been a better time to sell a home on your own via the online, as a digital home seller formerly a by owner (FSBO) method. In this day and age, there are very few reasons why someone would need to pay a traditional real estate agent an inflated 5-7% commission fee to sell their home. And the FSBO method offers sellers a variety of options, including full service, self-direct and limited service all of which can accommodate the private home seller. But before we dive into "the how" the decision whether or not to sell your own home is an easy one to make —yes, you should sell your home through an alterative, for-sale-by-owner model and save thousands in the process. Paying a 5-7% commission in today's market is just throwing money away.

Whether you are selling to downsize, expand, relocate, as a financial decision, or any other reason, you can easily manage the sale of your home with the wealth of information available and new online business models. We as consumers have become empowered, and have access to so much key information including pricing, demographics, documents, marketing and more, empowering you to successfully sell your own real estate, on your terms and under your control with favorable economics. The information that was once privileged and available only to licensed real estate agents is now out there for everyone, which is one reason that the traditional real estate agent sales method should be a thing of the past. In today's market you are never alone and you have immediate access to local market participants depending on which model you work with (covered in Chapter 6). At sites such as DwellOwner.com, we provide a full-service offering to assist home sellers through the whole process — from listing to closing, and completely avoiding the traditional sell-side commission.

The financial benefits of selling as an informed homeowner are obvious and monumental, and can save you double-digit earnings on the return of your cash investment. For example, if you purchased your home for $400,000 and put 20% down, that's an $80,000 initial cash investment. Let's say a year later you decide to sell you home for $400,000, but do so by utilizing a tradition real estate agent. You would have to pay a 6% real estate commission, which amounts to a $24,000 price tag for doing business. That's $24,000 stripped away from your return, or 30% ($24,000 divided by $80,000) of your hard-earned equity, as shown below. Even if your home sold for an increase amount, let's say $435,000, you would still lose 21% of your equity if you were using a traditional real estate agent. And this example does not take into consideration all of the maintenance, tax, principal and interest payments you made, along with the time value of money that would show an even higher loss. Why give away 21 to 30% of you sale price on top of all that?

In the U.S., real estate brokerage fees tally up at over $60 billion on an annual basis, and the industry is stripping away billions in equity and savings from everyday consumers. Despite the dramatic increase in home values, and the advances in technology that now provide consumers with access to a wealth of information, this is a model that hasn't changed in decades. We'll get why a little later.

The Real Cost of Real Estate Commissions

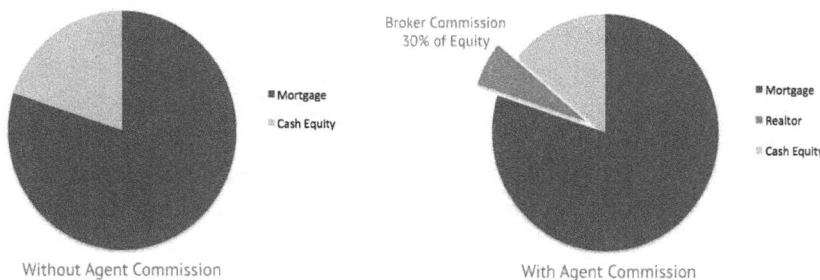

Without Agent Commission | With Agent Commission

Let's also consider the general caliber and experience of agents in the real estate market. It's easy for almost anyone to become a real estate agent; selling an actual home, however is a different story. It's estimated that over 30% of the two million agents in the U.S. are not able to sell even one home annually. By listing with an agent, with an exclusive, you are putting yourself and your future at the mercy of said agent's talent and track record and at a steep price. And who knows your home better than you do? With the DIY online tools available today, you can market your home more favorably on your own, with ease and simplicity, to gain maximum market exposure. Even if you list with a "top producer," your home is one of many listings they have secured and you most likely won't get the attention and service you deserve. You, the homeowner, know your product (your home) best and can speak of the attributes of your property, better than a third-party agent could. That's why **approximately 80% of all homes sell through a second party, not a listing agent.**

When you look across the traditional real estate brokerage space, one of the primary responsibilities is to recruit and retain licensed real estate agents. During my years in the brokerage space and driving product development for an online platform, I personally interviewed hundreds of agents at all levels. The common denominator was that, regardless of whether an agent sold a few hundred homes or one on an annual basis, they pretty much all did the same thing once they secured a listing: put up a yard sign, installed a lockbox and created a multiple listing service entry outside of modest offline advertising in local print newspapers (yes, some still run ads) and other publications. The commission rates are driven by the broker (regardless of whether they were independent or part of a real estate franchise) so agents were trained and versed on how to overcome objections and to justify the inflated real estate commission fees of 5-7% on average. They never competed on price, or rarely went below 5%.

Once I met with a regional top producer at one of the larger franchise brands. He wanted to meet with me to explore what we could offer and I was interested in learning more about his business practices. He was well dressed in a suit and definitely leveraged the current archaic system that allowed him to exploit consumers. He owned a fleet of Mercedes, Italian shoes and custom-made suits. He earned between $750,000 and $1,000,000 in gross commissions, year after year. On another occasion I met with different agent who just had just gotten her license and was trying out a new career. Despite being brand-new, this agent charged the same commission rate as the top producer and offered the same "value" proposition. The top producer did more to promote his personal brand with TV shows, commercials and more, but their approach to selling homes was fairly comparable.

The top producer was formerly a bank teller and the new agent was a mom who took several years off from her previous career to raise her family and wanted a new career that provided flexibility now that she was a single mother. None of this is surprising as the caliber of agents varies greatly across the industry, with low barriers of entry. In a way, it's a lot like the California gold rush; basically anyone with dreams of achieving a quick fortune can try it out with little or no credentials of any kind. Fortunately now, with alternative real estate models like DwellOwner, a seller can get the same — if not more — exposure and advisory services to sell their home at a fraction of the cost, with a fixed fee upfront or percentage of sale at closing that is significantly lower than traditional real estate firms.

Overall, the entire real estate brokerage industry is inefficient, with low barriers of entry for agents. There is no real way to accurately measure competency with the industry and the wrong metrics (sales) are what's used to determine an agent's value.

Over the past few years, new online business models that provide a wealth of resources and advisory services from listing to close, and are designed to offer full services at modest cost, have become available. They help non-professionals with pricing, signage, document drafting, negotiating and more, all at a fixed fee, paid prior to or at closing, depending on the package that's selected. The older FSBO model lured people to their site with a "free" postings that were similar to a classified advertisement, only to upsell you to a flat fee multiple listing service and other items like yard signs, a flier box, lockbox and more. That's where the service ended and most sellers who used these types of services ended up with an unsuccessful sale.

But today, there are some great reasons why you should seriously consider selling your home outside of a traditional real estate model with commission fees. Is the licensed real estate agent who just put up a sign in your front yard really worth thousands for the services they provided? NO. Therefore, if you are a seller that already has your home listed, you should seriously consider exiting the listing agreement selling your home on your own.

What if my home is currently on the market with a licensed real estate agent?

It's simple — request an unconditional withdrawal form from your agent (they should have one available through the local MLS, which provides the standard forms and documents most agents use day-to-day.) You are not being forced at gunpoint to give away potentially 20% or more of your home equity to someone who's simply going to put your home in the MLS, snap some photos on their iPhone and provide a yard sign with a lockbox. Approximately 80% of all homes sell by through a third-party buyer agent, not the listing agent, and yet you'll be on the hook for a 5 -7% total commission of charge, with 3% going to the buyer's agent. This sounds even more ridiculous when you consider that the role of the listing agent can be done better by you, the informed and prepared home seller.

Unfortunately, if you have already listed with an agent, your listing agreement may or may not have conditions to release you from the contract until it expires. I know of a situation with one informed homeowner who paid a brokerage's advertising expenses (a few hundred dollars) as a trade-off to be released from her listing. She realized that she would still save over $10,000 in real estate commissions in exchange for the modest spend to secure the release. Listing agreements differ depending on who or what firm is handling the listing, be sure to pay attention to the details when considering exiting an existing listing agreement with an agent.

Unconditional withdrawal / release is when the listing agency releases the sellers from all obligations defined in the listing agreement including rights to commission during the "Broker Protection Clause" time period. You can re-list the house with another real estate agency OR sell it privately and not be responsible for commission.

Conditional withdrawal means that there is a "protection clause" for a specific time period in the listing agreement (typically 3 months from expiration of the listing agreement which remains in effect even after the withdrawal.

Effective Pricing

Correctly pricing your home is one of the most important tasks when selling. The good news is that today, independent home sellers can easily access online data to ensure that they are pricing their home at a fair market value. In Chapter 3, I walk you through different methodologies and approaches, along with alternative online models like DwellOwner, which provides valuation guidance as part of its home listing packages along with an interactive valuation tool on the site.

There are several online resources to explore when pricing your home, such as alternative valuation models (AVMs), which allow you to enter your address to calculate a price by looking at recent market activity and other variables. Another effective tool is a comparative market analysis (CMA), which historically were prepared by a licensed real estate agent. Most for-sale-by-owner models now offer this service to home sellers and, if not, there is nothing stopping you from reaching out to a local listing agent to have them prepare one for you — they will be more than happy to do it for free with the anticipation of listing your home. Depending on the online platform you have chosen to work with to sell your home, it's included as part of the flat fee. Home sellers can perform a CMA directly on DwellOwner, where you have access to the same tools to generate one independently on your home. The data is pulled from the MLS allowing you to compare active, pending and sold properties while making any necessary adjustments to derive at a listing price for your home.

Market Exposure

Ultimately, an agent doesn't control market pricing and so their goal is to *drive* marketing in order to maximize exposure via the multiple listing services (MLS), which is where most homes sell. Once a home is on the MLS, it effectively puts every buyer's agent in the local market to work trying to sell a home. It's also the best way to make your home sells quickly. As I discuss in Chapter 5, it's important to understand *where* your home is being syndicated if you are seeking to maximize exposure to it.

> There has never been more favorable a time to sell your home privately than now, given the power of online consumer "DIY" platforms that make it easy for the average person (with no real estate experience) to sell their home by themselves and for a fraction of the cost of using a traditional real estate agent.

Traditional versus a Digital Home Seller Approach

The new digital home seller is empowered by our real estate community and supportive market participants on Dwell Owner. Their approach targets the nearly 100% of online buyers to maximize market exposure and allows home sellers to partner with a full service hybrid real estate brokerage model that empowers consumers and saves them thousands in real estate commission expense.

Traditional FSBO Seller		**Digital Home Seller**
Classified newspaper ads	=>	Online syndication
Open houses	=>	Virtual, 24/7 open houses
Selling privately, not using a full service online real estate platform	=>	Having agents do the work for you
It's just you and your agent (and whatever experience they may have)	=>	A broad range of advisory services from listing to closing
Resources to reach buyers	=>	Cutting-edge resources from start to closing, and advisory services throughout
Limited access to forms – agent is your gatekeeper	=>	Access to all MLS/state transaction forms and disclosures
Flier stands and yard signs	=>	Online syndication
Flat-fee MLS or pure FSBO	=>	Hybrid, full-service offerings (such as what's available at DwellOwner.com)
Q&A limited to agent answers and info	=>	Online crowd-sourced questions and answers via dwellowner.com and the digitalhomeseller.co
Home staging	=>	Optimized online staging
Photography	=>	Video walk-through and professional photography

Chapter Summary

Yes, you can and *should* sell your own home as a for sale by owner (FSBO) because:
- The savings, on average, are at least 3% of list price;
- The real loss of listing with a traditional agent is 5-7%, which is a big hit to your cash-on-cash return.
- Market dynamics and trends all indicate that selling your own home independently is easier and more cost effective than ever.
- The game has changed for home sellers, primarily with your marketing approach and selecting a platform to use, like DwellOwner.com.
- Online display and presentation is imperative - use professional photos and video.
- Optimize online staging and price accordingly.

2
THE INDUSTRY LANDSCAPE – DESIGNED FOR THE DIGITAL HOME SELLER

It's important to understand the behavior of homebuyers in order to successfully sell your own home, and how the right marketing channels can gain maximum exposure for your home. Billions of dollars have been invested in researching the home discovery process and buyer attitudes. Today's online real estate platforms leverage this investment in order to easily attract qualified buyers.

Today's consumer is more digitally connected than ever, enjoying more access to and deeper engagement with content and brands through a variety of multiple connected devices that can be used almost anywhere. Home buyers now search online to find a home, and are able to do when it's most convenient. Buyers who search for a home online have access to a vast array of information, including available inventory, recent sales, demographics, school ratings and more, right from their mobile device or tablet. The home discovery process has become increasingly digital, and the majority of home buyers begin the search for a home online, six months prior to contacting an agent. By the time a buyer does contact an agent, most have already narrowed down their search and are typically interested in using the agent to access properties in which they are interested. The digital process stops when the home buyer is forced to resort to using an agent, who literally holds the keys and controls access to the property listed on the MLS.

Here's a bit of history on the MLS —it's lagging infrastructure is embarrassing when compared with that of other industries. Imagine searching for a vacation online on Expedia or Orbitz, finding the dream vacation for your family, narrowing down the hotel, airfare, and even excursions for your trip, and then being told you are now beholden to a travel agent in order to execute everything, and that the travel agent will be charging you a commission for their "services". This is the current state of the real estate industry. It's experienced growth in innovation and efficiency around the discovery process, but everything comes to a halt after that. There have been some attempts to offer a streamlined, end-to-end solution for the industry, but nothing that is mainstream (or not riddled with complications) currently exists.

While I was a senior executive at an online real estate platform that was developed by a large, publicly-traded company, we sold over 120,000 distressed homes online, and interested consumers could only bid or place offers on the properties listed on online. We also piloted several programs for the retail market (non-distressed) with similar, lukewarm success. Given agent behavior, product friction and the traditional brokerage mindset, the deals from the site would ultimately be forced go offline after the initial search, bid and offer phase, despite the consumer's willingness to remain online. They just had not been able to develop a platform that could offer a complete, streamlined process. We also had one kind of unfair competitive advantage: our largest client was a mortgage servicer that owned nearly all of the properties listed on our site, so the company could influence the market and steer traffic to our platform with standardized terms. Basically, if a prospective home buyer found a home listed on the site, they could either work with an agent or submit an offer independently through an auction or non-auction process.

There is no doubt the real estate industry has changed significantly over the past decade. A recent study by the National Association of Realtors (NAR) stated that in 1964, 40% of home buyers read newspaper ads to find a home and 7% drove around looking for an open house.[1] In comparison, today nearly 100% of consumers search online, and despite this fact, many agents and brokerages are still using the archaic methods from 1964. On the rare occasions when I do have a newspaper in my hands, I still see advertisements for homes being funded by traditional real estate firms, including listing from the largest franchises. There are even open houses being advertised, when in reality, less than 9% of consumers actually find their home by attending an open house.[2]

As consumers are the ones who have reshaped the process of home discovery via online methods, sellers who want to be successful should and can effectively target qualified buyers with ease by using a cost-effective, alternative real estate model.

> Recent independent real estate market studies have shown that most consumers would not only be willing to make a real estate purchase online, but that they have come to expect this should be a reality in the near future, given how other industries have been transformed this way. This, combined with new industry entrants, should finally accelerate change while driving pressure on the current real estate commission model.

The Digital Consumer & General Online Market Trends –The Amazon Analogy

Digital disruption continues to upend retail. Today, global consumers are more empowered than ever and have access to a wealth of information, while brick and mortar retailers are struggling to remain relevant. The speed of technology adoption has raised the stakes for both retailers and their consumer packaged goods partners, and we are also (finally!) seeing this in real estate as well.

Currently, retail ecommerce sales are at about $1.7 trillion globally and $340 billion in the U.S alone, and these figures are forecasted to continue to grow aggressively, especially across mobile devices.[3] As for real estate, more than 5 million homes have been sold annually in the U.S., which has been the average for the past few years. At the peak in 2007 over 7 million residential single-family homes were sold in a single year. Current inventory levels remain low, with pricing increases seen in most markets over the last year.

These numbers are important, but so is the fact that business models have changed, putting consumers in a position of control. For example, Amazon exceeded $100 billion in revenue in fiscal year 2015, according to their public 10K filings with the Securities Exchange Commission. As the world's largest online retailer, Amazon sells a number of categories of goods, including books, electronics, groceries, jewelry and even auto parts. The company is also an ecommerce and Internet technology platform, a fulfillment and logistics platform, a search technology, an Internet advertising platform, and even an Internet startup incubator. Amazon built an online retail business around three goals:

- **Best prices:** Amazon products are generally offered at a discount (a steep discount in the case of books). This is now *finally* being done in the real estate brokerage industry, as full service aligns with the best prices through alternative, hybrid, real-estate brokerage models. Historically, for sale by owner (FSBO) offerings were very limited and rigid, and did not provide the home seller with much other than access to the MLS, a yard sign and other ancillary items like contracts and flier boxes.

- **Unrivaled selection:** Amazon often has the largest selection of goods in a particular category, especially books. In the real estate world, Amazon's wide selection can be compared to a full-service offering or to how some brokerage models unbundle services through an à la carte menu of options. Others, such as DwellOwner, include everything in a fixed fee. As I discuss in Chapter 6, some self-direct, online real estate sites charge home sellers a low price to sign up and then charge separately for advising and other services, landing you at a higher price point in the end.

- **Convenience**: Amazon focuses on the customer and tries to make all purchases an easy and enjoyable online experience. In the real estate sector, consumers can now search for a home anytime from their mobile, laptop or desktop device, viewing photos, virtual tours and more. Whether the home search is being conducted at 2AM or 2PM, consumers have access to the same available inventory at a push of a button. This information was once only available to licensed real estate agents. The listing data in the MLS has been exposed to the consumer, eliminating the need to use a real estate agent to search for a home.

The pressure Amazon put on traditional models like Barnes & Noble was significant, and not unlike what Netflix did to Blockbuster, by offering digital movies that are accessible from home or almost anywhere, with the best prices and a broad selection of titles. Today, unless it's a new release that's currently in theaters, you can rent or purchase almost any movie without leaving your home. I remember walking across the street from my apartment building in Manhattan about a decade ago to pick out movies at Blockbuster. My wife and I would walk to the store that was nearest to us (they were everywhere!), scan titles manually by walking up down different aisles, hoping the store had an available copy of the movie we wanted to watch and looking over the shoulders of other consumers before we could check out at the cashier. All this, with the added inconvenience of having to return our movie selections within 24 hours or be responsible for late fees for each day we were late. Wow, just looking back on how inefficient that process was compared to how we watch movies at home today is tiring! Now, as digital consumers of movies, we can search by several different categories right from our living room and everything is included in one monthly price. Even if we switch over to Amazon for select movie titles, we still only pay a modest cost and the convenience is a one-click process from any one of our online devices.

The same comparison can be made to the travel, stock trading, tax preparation and so many other industries where technology has changed the competitive landscape, and has transformed the way these businesses function, while driving efficiency and transparency for the consumer. Technology blew open the traditional pricing models of these industries, successfully driving overall costs down while creating a better user experience. The same is *finally* happening across the real estate sector, despite the industry establishment trying to prevent the inevitable through unfair and unethical practices (see Chapter 11) that include creating market friction and resistance. These changes are long overdue, however, there are even attempts by franchises and large independent regional brokerage firms to create a separate MLS to control home data and who can access it through a project called Upstream. Personally, I believe this project will be unsuccessful and view it as more of a distraction for the industry. The good news is that there are other players out there who are committed to innovation and advancing the real estate industry in the same way that so many other industries have benefited.

> An informed home seller can get the same full service to sell their home at a fraction of the cost using sites like DwellOwner. The consumer is driving change and the traditional real estate brokers and agents are trying to adapt to justify their existence, as their roles are redefined in the home buying and selling process.

In the spring of 2014 while my family and I were living Luxembourg, we decided to take in impromptu trip to Barcelona, not realizing that virtually all of Europe had the same intention. When we were about halfway there in France, my wife and I used our mobile phone in an attempt to secure a hotel room — which was when we learned that there were no rooms available in the city. (One of the things that drove my wife crazy when we lived in Europe was not planning our excursions in advance and just venturing out with the family. In this particular case, she had a point.) Thankfully, we used a handy mobile app — Hotel Tonight — to reserve a room with modest accommodations with minimal effort. Using my travel worn phone with a cracked screen, we searched for a hotel room throughout an area of roughly 400 miles, through different towns and communities, and found a suitable place to rest so that we could continue our journey in the morning. Having already traveled over ten hours with two kids under the age of ten in tow, finding a room at 2AM was invaluable for the state of our marriage and for the start of our vacation. I suppose if things had worked out differently, I could have used one of the several digital dating apps that exist. Technology has truly impacted all industries!

One of my favorite examples of an industry that has been transformed through the adoption of technology is the travel industry. Unlike the real estate industry, where innovation has historically been concentrated only on the home discovery process, the travel industry has fully adapted itself to the digital consumer and has driven innovation across the entire process of how we shop for and purchase travel services. Independent platforms (those that are not affiliated with travel industry, such as Expedia and the now long forgotten TravelZoo) gained market share because they empowered the consumer to independently plan any type of travel and shop for the most competitive prices. In 2001, the travel industry responded by creating an alliance that led to the formation of Orbitz. Orbitz grew out of what was once a partnership between major airlines, and was subsequently owned by several entities before it was acquired by Expedia in February of 2015 for $1.2 billion. The traditional players in the travel industry united to create a competing brand, with new, innovative, consumer-facing platforms to meet the needs of the newly minted digital consumer and to avoid being made obsolete by utilizing the same, archaic business models that had been used in the industry for decades. We are JUST now seeing this in the real estate industry — more than a decade later — but instead of going with the revolution, the major real estate industry players are trying to thwart progress by attempting to control access to relevant data (MLS active listings).

Before Orbitz began operating, the company faced intense antitrust scrutiny, because five of the six "major" airlines were collaborating on the project and thus collectively controlled 80% of the US air travel market at the time. Several consumer organizations, as well as Orbitz's primary competitors, spent significant amounts of money lobbying the United State Department of Transportation to block the project from the outset, and some 23 state attorneys general also voiced concerns due to the complaints of local competitors. Despite these effort, Orbitz was ultimately given the go-ahead.

Ironically, before Orbitz was acquired by Expedia in 2015, the company was first acquired in 2004 by Cendent, a company that now goes by the name Realogy. Realogy owns the largest real estate brands in the industry, including Sotheby's, Coldwell Banker, ERA, Century 21 and Better Homes and Gardens. In 2006, Apollo, which is one of the largest private equity firms in existence, acquired the real estate assets from Realogy which tells us numerous entities recognized the value of what was essentially a travel industry mafia.

Today, the real estate industry's traditional franchises and large regional players are trying to come together to create a competing platform, just like the airlines that came together to create Orbitz in 2001. Despite Zillow and Trulia's current dominant market share, the big industry players are pushing an initiative called Upstream. I provide more details about this in Chapter 11. Once again, I have very little confidence in ability of the old guard to execute a project such as this at this stage, which, by the way, is about ten years too late.

Real Estate Investment & Innovation

As noted earlier in the chapter, most innovation to date in the residential real estate sector has been centered on the home discovery process, with monetization built around the licensed agent and third party ancillary providers. Investment in the real estate tech sector increased from $24 million in 2012 to more $1.5 billion in 2015 in effort to drive efficiency in the marketplace.[1]

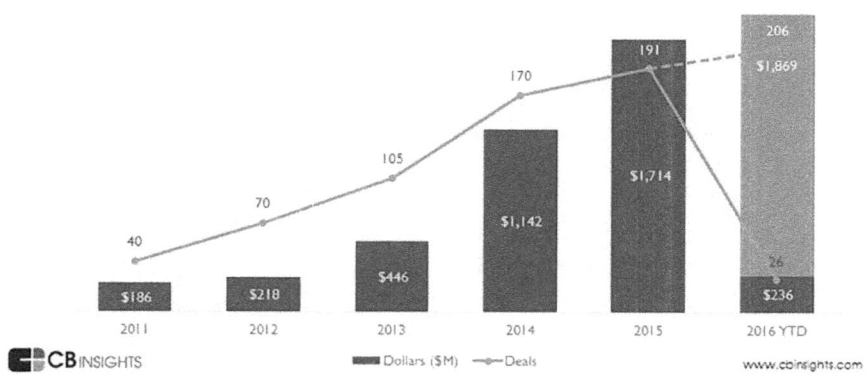

Real Estate Tech Financing History: Deals And Dollars
2011 - 2016 YTD (2/16/2016)

I classify real estate investment as involving the home discovery process, property viewing, transaction processes and closing. Some newer models are trying to redefine the transaction and closing process to drive automation and efficiency with pre-vetted homes that can be purchased online and close within a timely manner. Pre-vetting streamlines most of the closing requirements, including valuation, title and closing services. Companies like DwellOwner offer reduced costs and enhanced services through its full-service home seller offering. Other new, exciting areas of innovation are reviewed in Chapter 13, where we expect further investment to challenge the industry processes and drive efficiency include blockchain, artificial intelligence and virtual reality. These technologies have the potential to further minimize the role of a traditional real estate agent and empower the digital home seller.

The online home discovery process is coming even more easy to use, as consumer-driven platforms are upping the ante by providing data based on lifestyle factors, community and offering other data points such as commuting times so that users can personalize their search to match homes that suit their wants and needs. This is light years away from the traditional home search method, where consumers could only look for homes with limited search criteria, that typically included simply the location, price, and number of bedrooms and bathrooms that were desired.

Investment capital has historically concentrated on the home discovery process, so the digital home seller is positioned favorably to capitalize on market infrastructure to gain maximum market exposure easily with online syndication once their home is placed on the market. Hundreds of millions of dollars have been invested in the home search process over the past decade by companies with billion-dollar market caps. This allows you to reach prospective homebuyers with minimum effort, given these companies' spend and market reach. Home sellers are no longer force into to using a traditional agent to posting a listing on a secure MLS system, because the screen with the MLS data has been turned around for all consumers to access, no unlike what the airline industry did with flight reservations. Do you remember having to connect with a travel agent in order to gain access to flight information? Even if you don't, can you imagine having to or wanting to do so now? Now, in real estate you can do the very same thing: self-manage the entire process including search, price, and reserve on your own.

> The best and easiest way to sell a home is to drive demand by maximizing market exposure so that your listing gets in front of a great number of interested and qualified buyers. To date, consumers are more empowered to sell their own home now than ever before, due to the technology that exists and the proclivity of the digital home-buyer with access to a wealth of information.

Platforms such as DwellOwner.com, pre-qualify buyers before providing them access to a home for sale, depending on which listing package a home seller selects. Regardless, as a private seller, it's imperative that your home is syndicated to all the leading real estate websites to maximize your market exposure. This includes the MLS, where your listing should originate. Once a home is on the MLS, it is typically syndicated to Zillow, Trulia, Realtor.com and others, which provides visibility to broad range of home shoppers. In today's market, it's advisable to use one the several alternative models that exist to avoid being charged a sell-side commission. An alternative model would be a full service real estate brokerage offering, providing you professional advisory support throughout the process while avoiding paying a traditional listing commission.

In *The Digital House Hunt,* which is a study that was conducted by Google and the National Association of Realtors (NAR) a few years ago, it was reported that homebuyers' stats are growing exponentially, confirming what many in the industry already knew. Real estate-related searches on Google have increased over 250% over the past four years alone. Mobile search engines are used by 89% of home buyers, who want real-time, accurate information when conducting a home search.

Source: Google & Compete Home Shopper Mobile Survey, 2012

Given the current industry landscape, a consumer can easily place their own home on the market online which maximizes exposure. Again, this process typically begins by listing the home on the MLS, from where it is then syndicated across a number of real estate websites.

Profile of a Homebuyer – Select Industry Stats

In the past, first-time buyers comprised about 40% of homebuyers; however, NAR data indicates that this number has trended downward since 2011 and currently sits at 32%. While married couples represent the largest group of home buyers (currently 67%), single females represent the second-largest group of buyers (currently 15%) although this number has dropped from a high of 22% in 2006.

- In 2015, the average homebuyer was age 44, and had a median household income of $86,100. The median age of first-time homebuyers was 31 years old.
- Buyers typically search for a duration of ten weeks and consider ten homes, according to NAR.
- Homeowners, on average, own a home for a duration that ranges between 5-7 years.

Source: National Association of Realtors

Largest Sub Sector - Millennials

It is predicted that Millennials, or Gen Y, (those born between 1980 – 2000) will become the generation with the greatest spending power by 2017 and will be one of the largest sub-sectors in the U.S.; representing an estimated to 80–90 million people. Due to its size and digital behavior, Gen Y will have a strong impact on the real estate industry. They are poised to reshape the economy, expected to change the ways we buy and sell, and thus it's anticipated that companies will be forced to re-examine how they do business in order to accommodate Millennials.

Gen Y will have a big impact on the real estate sector as well, which is a little ironic as the average age of a realtor is around 58 years old. Only 3% of agents are under the age of 30 and most of the other 97% of the agent population is not adept at conducting business the way that Millenials do, which is by doing almost everything from their mobile devise. The real estate brokerage industry has to revise traditional practices to remain relevant. Millennials are technology efficient and value driven, and therefore are perfectly suited for online hybrid real estate models. They are doing most of the work themselves, comparable to the broader market searching for homes online, using their mobile device to access information.

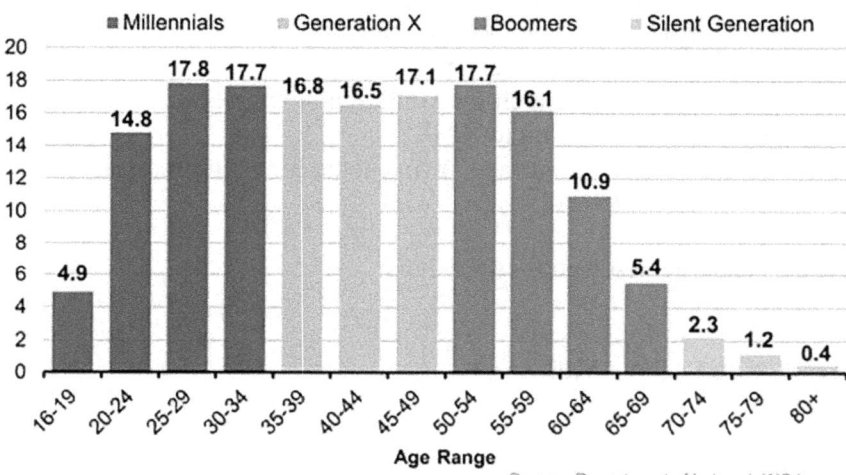

As a home seller, you will want to appeal to this segment – which will collectively have some of the strongest buying power in decades and position your home online in order to capture their interest. As they get older, Millennials and look to settle down, and as employment improves, this generation will invest more heavily in real estate. I have included a few tips on reaching this important demographic in Chapter 5.

Social Media – Influence Shopping Behavior

Consumers in the digital age are influenced by social media more than anything. They are active in sharing opinions online, this has social media traffic growing faster than any other channels. The internet has over 3 billion users with 2.3 billion active social media users, each with an average of 5.54 social media accounts. That could be Facebook, Twitter, Linkedin, Instagram, SnapChat, WhatsApp, Youtube and more!

Social Channel Users

Facebook	1.65 billion
Youtube	> 1 billion
SnapChat	> 100 million
WhatsApp	900 million
Linkedin	364 million
Twitter	320 million

Social media is used among most demographic groups, but use is especially fervent among millennials. A recent report issued by Deloitte found that 47% of millennials are influenced in their purchases by social media, compared to 19% for all other age groups.

The Deloitte report also provided some insight into which product categories work best on social media. According to their data, 56% of consumers buying baby products are influenced by social media, compared to 40% for home furnishings, 33% for health and wellness, and 32% for automotive.

The impact of social media is not something the real estate industry can afford to overlook. Consumers who use social media during their shopping process are four times more likely to spend more on purchases than those who do not. Additionally, the report found that shoppers are 29% more likely to make a purchase the same day when using social media before or during a trip to the store.

As a home seller, you want to not only partner with an online platform to maximize exposure, but also engage with your social network to share with them your home is for sale. You can ask your friends to post on Facebook, retweet and like your listing as well.

Chapter Summary

1. Home sellers have access to a number of tools to reach qualified buyers and an informed self-seller will have greater reach than a traditional agent.
2. The digital consumer is fueling the success and number of for-sale-by-owner listings, increasing the number of users — which is already at 1.5 million —who sell privately every year.
3. Despite overwhelming consumer online trends across other sectors and in real estate, traditional real estate franchises and regional firms are attempting to limit access to information. One way is through a project called Upstream. I view this is as a mere distraction, as other marketplaces already have mindshare in the market. The consumer will win.
4. To date, real estate innovation has concentrated on the home discovery phase. This allows you to tap into these platforms that provide this service in order to leverage their spend to reach qualified home buyers.
5. Home buyer profiles of today validate the notion that people are conducting home searches independently, before even considering an agent.
6. Technology is changing the industry and low-cost hybrid models like DwellOwner will become the norm within a few years, once home sellers become more market-aware because they save sellers money and just make sense!

3
LIST PRICE – METHODS & CONSIDERATIONS

Accurate pricing is imperative to the successful sale of your home, regardless of whether it's listed with a traditional agent or an alternative online real estate platform.

A recent study by the National Association of Realtors (NAR) found that pricing is one of the most difficult tasks for private sellers. I believe it's one of the easiest aspects of selling your home if you are a digitally-empowered consumer, although it is still critical to do it correctly.

Accurate pricing is imperative for a successful home sale. Even if you're in a hurry to sell and price isn't your main concern, you still need a baseline at which to start marketing your home. One thing is for sure: Pricing is one of the biggest decisions in the selling process. Set your home too high and you run the risk of scaring off potential buyers. Many people won't even consider looking at a house, even in a very desirable location, if it's out of their price range. An over-inflated price also means your house will not compare favorably with other similarly priced homes. Even worse, buyers may not even see your listing when they search online if your home price falls outside of their search parameters.

The average real estate agent in the U.S. sells only on a few homes per year, if any and through their MLS they are able to cover a broad section of market territory that can sometimes be several counties in size. Home values are impacted by location and several other variables. When you contact an agent to run a comparative market analysis (CMA), a comparison of active, pending and sold properties pulled from the MLS, they try to determine a value before speaking with you to make any adjustments to price that will most benefit themselves. No one knows your home, neighborhood and local amenities better than you. Therefore, with access to a number of online tools that provide you with the ability to pull the same (if not better) information, you will be able to set the appropriate market price for your home better than anyone else.

It's also important to be responsive to market conditions and have a game plan in place for when your home goes on the market. For example, if your home doesn't have any showings in the first 30 days, perhaps consider a price reduction. The general rule of thumb is that the first 4-6 weeks on the market are the most important, so not having any showings is a strong indicator that you need to reduce the price. Ultimately, your home is worth what the market is willing to pay for it. One method to calculate market performance is through market absorption, which is the rate at which inventory is selling in your local market. You will want to know how homes in your area and price range are selling. A balanced market is typically 5 - 6 months and anything below is a seller's market and above would be considered a buyer's market.

Market Absorption Scale (Absorption Rate in Months)

Copyrighted Material

> **Absorption rate** is the rate at which available homes are sold in a specific real estate market during a given time period. It is calculated by dividing the total number of available homes by the average number of sales per month.

Valuation Methodologies

There are three primary valuation methods that can be used. One method is to have a licensed real estate agent prepare a comparative market analysis (CMA) to look at the most recent sold, active and pending sales in your neighborhood to determine a value (while taking into consideration your home's attributes in order to make any necessary adjustments.) The second primary valuation method is an automated valuation methodology (AVM), where you can enter your address online and the AVM will run an algorithm, that scans recent sales price and other variables to determine a value. The final valuation method to consider is hiring a licensed appraiser to set a value for your property. The appraiser basically uses the same approach (comparable sales) as someone doing a CMA. As a private seller, you have access to all of the above to generate a sale price for your home. I expect AVMs to be the norm going forward, as access to data and other sources of current information provides greater value than the average real estate agent.

For example, there are several sources online that can help you assign a valuation to your home via an AVM, including DwellOwner. If you're not confident about your research, requesting a CMA from one or more local agents is also an option. Historically, real estate agents have offered CMAs for free as marketing tools and home sellers are under no obligation to use an agent from whom they have requested a CMA. The worst thing that can happen is that the agent will decline to run the CMA. Who knows, the agent might even have the perfect buyer for your house! Lastly, you may also opt for a home appraisal which, depending on the size of your home and local market, can cost anywhere from $350 - $800.

As noted earlier, on <u>DwellOwner</u>, a homeowner can run a CMA directly on our site to assist them in deriving at a valuation. This is in addition to having our professional licensed staff providing guidance throughout the process.

Some Points for Consideration

When pricing a home, establishing an asking price is part science and part art, and there are several things you should consider.

- **Market Comparables.** This is the starting point for any thoughtful and successful pricing strategy; think of it as the "science" part. Take the time to study past sale statistics for homes in your area and areas similar to yours. None will be identical, of course, but having a clear understanding of true market value is the first step in establishing your list price. You can use sites like Zillow, Realtor.com and others to look at recent sales.

- **Competition.** While active listings have not yet sold, they can shed some light on your market competition. It is important to be aware of the competition's pricing, even though their numbers are often just an indication of the price at which your home will not sell. If there are several homes for sale in your neighborhood, you may want to consider pricing yours slightly below the competition to attract buyers. If there is limited inventory with high demand, you can be more aggressive. Regardless, when pricing your home, keep in mind that they amount that you come down may be equal to or greater than your carrying cost.

- **Do not overprice your home because you have "time."** There are many sellers who will start the listing process with an aggressively high price. Statistically, the best offers usually come in within the first three weeks, so listing too highly, even in the beginning, can cause a seller to miss out on a segment of qualified buyers. If the market is appreciating this strategy may work, but if prices in your area are declining and you price your home too high, you may quickly find yourself chasing a market and in turn costing yourself money. And if the market is stable, your home may sit on the market, costing you money and time.

- **Leave some room for negotiation, but don't overreach.** No seller wants to feel like he left money on the table and no buyer wants to overpay. Your sale price should give both parties room to maneuver, but if it is too high you risk being perceived as unrealistic and potential buyers will pass over your home.

- **Look at your home from a buyer's perspective.** Identify and promote those attributes of your home that will appeal to most families: a private yard, modern kitchen, finished basement, etc. Maybe the school bus stop is right in front of your house and there is public transportation just down the street? Any one of these things can make the difference in a buyer choosing your home over another listing.

- **Be responsive to market feedback and activity.** If your home is on the market and it is not being shown or if you receive feedback that you are priced too aggressively, adjust your sale price.

I expect AVMs and consumer driven CMA's to be the preferred choice for pricing assistance as we continue to move forward with making better data available across the board.

Today, home sellers are able to run an automated valuation and adjust for comparables and other factors and derive a price in seconds or minutes from their mobile device. Sellers no longer need an agent to show up with a binder or a PDF with comps pulled from their MLS. In 2016, YOU can easily be better informed than an agent and can come up with a better price for your home by yourself. You can obtain this information independently and depending on the service partner you select, a valuation may even be included.

Regardless of pricing method that you choose, general studies show that the first two weeks of your listing are the most critical to your success. Realize that as a private seller you are saving 3% of the list-side commission, so leave room to negotiate. During these initial days your home will be exposed to all active buyers. If your price is perceived as too high, you will quickly lose this initial audience and find yourself relying only on the trickle of new buyers entering the market each day. Markets are dynamic, and with access to an abundance of information you have never been better informed and armed to price your home effectively.

Chapter Summary

1. There are several online sources you can use to research recently sold properties on public portals like Realtor.com, Zillow and others.
2. Establish your home's market value accurately *before* putting your home on the market.
3. A number of AVMs are available for free and agents are always eager to do a CMA, although if you list with a model like DwellOwner, this service is included.
4. Research active and sold listings, know your competition and the market absorption rate for homes in your price range.
5. Be mindful not to overprice your home initially, as the first few weeks are when you statistically will attract the most exposure.

4
PREPARING YOUR HOME FOR SALE

Keep it simple, as you prepare your home for showings be mindful of which improvements will have the best return on investment (ROI). You can do it yourself. Balance offline with online!

This chapter is divided into two sections. The first reviews home preparation and includes a summary of which home modifications have the best return on investment. The second section focuses on managing expectations and understanding the current market climate. Is it a buyer's or seller's market? A seller's market means there are more buyers than inventory and this usually means you will get near or above asking price. If it's a buyer's market there is more inventory and the average number of days your house sits on the market may be longer.

It may seem like common sense to physically prepare your home to sell, although I can't tell you how many homes I have seen where best practices such as this were not considered. At the same time, some home sellers take the other extreme approach, taking on renovations, major projects and hiring outside professionals when it all could have been easily managed independently while saving a lot of money in the process. Follow these simple guidelines: prepare the interior and exterior of your home to maximize the effectiveness of your display; on the exterior, keep the grass cut, shrubs trimmed and home clean to maximize curb appeal as studies have shown that doing so can you more money for your home. Create a strong overall presentation.

> **Curb appeal** is defined as attractiveness or "wow" factor of the exterior of a residential or commercial property, as viewed from the street. Strong curb appeal goes a long way in helping to sell a home.

One agent we interviewed met an individual who was selling a high-end condominium that was over 6,000 square feet and loaded with amenities. Prior to the meeting, the sellers were prepared to hire professionals to manage several improvement projects. We were able to advise them on basic principles to minimize their spending in order to still get the highest price, as their initial investment was not targeted as areas that would generate the highest ROI. This chapter will explain these basic principles.

The Five Ds:
1. Declutter
2. Depersonalize
3. Disassociate
4. Damage
5. DwellOwner

Declutter
One of the first steps in the home staging process is to eliminate and all clutter. Clutter is anything that makes your home look small, cramped, disorganized, busy or untidy. Clutter can be too much furniture, too many photos, piles of mail, too many accessories or even clashing paint colors. Clutter is anything that might distract your buyer from seeing the good features of your home.

Decluttering can be overwhelming for even the most motivated among us. As such, it's important to approach the process systematically: room by room, surface by surface, wall by wall, closet by closet, drawer by drawer, removing anything that is not essential to the room's function.

Depersonalize
Once your home looks great and feels neat and organized it's time to depersonalize. Take a close look at the personalization of the space. Personalization is anything that makes your home distinctly yours and no one else's — the things your family and friends would identify as

unmistakably and uniquely yours. Think of it as your signature on your personal space. Personalization is anything that would make a buyer feel "this is not my home, it's theirs." For that very reason it's important to depersonalize the space without taking away from the warmth and style that make the home attractive, and giving prospective buyers the opportunity to visualize themselves living in your home.

This is probably the easiest part of preparing your home for market because it's relatively easy to identify. First, start with photos. Removing every photo from your home is not necessary. The single photo of you and your dog on a nightstand can be okay but if you are someone who loves to display a copious amount of photos and decorates with snapshots by the dozens you'll want to pare down significantly. The over-sized family photo above the mantle also should be taken down and put away until your home is sold. Aside from photos, be sure to put away any collection of items that are personal. Tuck away any of your children's artwork that may reside on your fridge as well.

Of course, your collectables aren't odd — we're speaking of other people's odd collectables! But collectibles are personal collections nonetheless. Matchbooks, stamps, shot glasses, vintage skateboard decks, avant guard art or sculpture, corks, bottles and cans, dolls, action figures and Hummel figurines all fall into this category. Not only are collections of such items highly personal, but they are distractions, just like personal photos. Your potential buyer may very well be a huge fan of those cute little German figurines but the last thing you want is your buyer skipping the home tour for a chance to explore your impressive collection.

Disassociate
This may be the hardest of the five D's, especially if you've raised a family in your home and have many fond memories there. When you disassociate yourself from the house it becomes the place where you live but is no longer your home. It no longer reflects your family, personality or views, but is ideally a clean slate that a buyer can emotionally work with to create their own attachments and memories. Disassociation is difficult because

we all have memories attached to possessions and putting them away can make us emotional and uncomfortable. So it's best to focus on your next adventure. The better job you do here disassociating, the faster you can connect with your next home and bring out all of your collections, personal items and photographs. And you'll always have your memories!

Buying a home is a largest investment, and therefore prospective buyers usually have a strong idea about the number of bedrooms, baths, square feet, etc. that they want. And there may be many homes in the current market which match your home's general description. **The key to successfully differentiating your home from the pack** is to remove distractions and build emotional bridges into the buyer's world that will cement the attraction. Staging is a big part of this.

Damage
In a standard purchase and sales contract there are inspection contingencies that typically allow for a home inspection, which is conducted by a licensed, third-party home inspector. Unfortunately, this is where deals sometimes do not move to closing; mostly because something is discovered and the buyers opt out of the contract, which is their legal if a satisfactory resolution cannot be reached.

I recommend having a home inspection done *prior* to putting your home on the market, which will serve two purposes: It will mitigate against any unforeseen issues and make your home more marketable. I elaborate on this further in Chapter 9.

I recommend that homeowners consider having an inspection done prior to putting their home on the market. This provides qualified buyers with reassurance and allows the seller to address any potential issues upfront, avoiding the risk of losing a buyer if a surprise issue surfaces and is not resolved.

DwellOwner

Not all paths may lead to DwellOwner (although I like to believe they do), but the point in referencing this platform is that it really is to your benefit to use a hybrid, full-service agency model that allows you to list your own home without paying a sell-side commission fee. The thousands you'll save in commission can be used to prepare your home for sale and address any items that may be damaged. Or to even buy something for your new home!

Which remodel has a higher ROI: bathroom or kitchen?

When investing in your home, it's important to be mindful of which renovation projects will allow you to recoup your investment. There are a number of sites online that provide market data, including the one below that shows which projects retain value at resale in 100 U.S. markets.

Midrange
2016 National Averages[1]

PROJECT	JOB COST	RESALE VALUE	COST RECOUPED
Attic Insulation (fiberglass)	$1,268	$1,482	116.9%
Backup Power Generator	$12,712	$7,556	59.4%
Basement Remodel	$68,490	$48,194	70.4%
Bathroom Addition	$42,233	$23,727	56.2%
Bathroom Remodel	$17,908	$11,769	65.7%
Deck Addition (composite)	$16,798	$10,819	64.4%
Deck Addition (wood)	$10,471	$7,850	75.0%
Entry Door Replacement (fiberglass)	$3,126	$2,574	82.3%
Entry Door Replacement (steel)	$1,335	$1,217	91.1%
Family Room Addition	$86,615	$58,807	67.9%
Garage Door Replacement	$1,652	$1,512	91.5%
Major Kitchen Remodel	$59,999	$38,938	64.9%
Manufactured Stone Veneer	$7,519	$6,988	92.9%
Master Suite Addition	$115,810	$74,224	64.1%
Minor Kitchen Remodel	$20,122	$16,716	83.1%
Roofing Replacement	$20,142	$14,446	71.7%
Siding Replacement	$14,100	$10,857	77.0%
Two-Story Addition	$171,056	$118,555	69.3%

Source: REMODELING magazine's 2016 Cost vs. Value Report

Chapter Summary

1. Use the five Ds: declutter, depersonalize, disassociate, damage and DwellOwner.
2. Consider which renovations or improvements will allow you to realize the highest ROI.
3. You are the most qualified to market and stage your home — no one knows your home better than you, not even the best real estate agent.
4. Keep it simple. Do the basics, which primarily consist of your time and energy, not money. Don't get caught up in taking on big projects that may eat into your return.
5. Use a hybrid full service real estate agency like DwellOwner that will avoid a sell-side commission – some of the savings could be reinvested in the home.

5
VIRTUAL HOME STAGING & SYNDICATION

Online presence and curb appeal should be the biggest priority when preparing a home to sell, along with positioning the home to gain the greatest visibility. **Optimize the impact of your virtual home staging** and market exposure through online syndication.

They say a picture is worth a thousand words, but when selling your home it can be worth thousands, literally. Today's buyers start their home search online, with over 94% of buyers searching for a home online before they ever contact an agent. Your home's listing photos are the first impression that a prospective buyer will have as they search market inventory online, so it's recommended that your listing photos are prepared professionally and arranged in such a way that tells a story, not just uploaded randomly. Think of listing photos as an invitation to your home. Despite how important this is, the industry seems to not get it, especially licensed real estate agents. I have seen listing photos with dogs, people, trash and other random items in sight, as well as photos taken in poor lighting and from bad angles.

Your home's photos need to be enticing. Think about what your reaction would be if you were shopping for a hotel room online and saw any of the things I listed above. You would move on and look for a room somewhere else! As the homeowner, depending on the online partner with which you work, you may be the one responsible for providing photos and other material (such as a walk-through video) to support your home's online display.

With models like DwellOwner, professional photos are included in a listing package and there are also a plethora of third-party services available if a home-seller wanted to take photos indecently.

Online virtual display requires more than just posting random pictures or posting a listing on a local real estate website. Buyers now look for video walk-throughs — soundless videos that can be shot directly from your mobile — that allow you to highlight a home's layout, landscape and key features that provide potential buyers with a feeling of what it's like being in a home. Video walk-throughs should be no longer than 1-2 minutes, so keep that in mind when putting one together. Most mobile phones have video capabilities so it's very easy to prepare and edit a video walk-through yourself.

> Cisco Systems, Inc. estimates that more than 80% of all internet traffic will be video by 2019.[1] In the U.S. the stats are even higher, at 85%. Over half of the world's population will have access to the internet by that time.

I recall meeting with the chief marketing officer of a luxury real estate brand and international auction house. Her message to the brand's agents was that photos would soon be supplanted by video, becoming the standard in the market. That was back in 2013, while she was correct, the real estate industry has been slow to adapt. However there's still great value, with smartphones and other advancements, in homeowners creating their own walk-through video and uploading it to the web for prospective buyers.

Video provides a 24/7 open house, allowing anyone who is shopping virtual access to your home at anytime. You can even host a live, real-time streaming open house on Facebook or Youtube. For example, with Facebook Live a homeowner can conduct a live open house for their entire social network, answering questions in real time with prospective buyers while selling the community attributes. I expect to see a surge in live streaming across the industry versus the traditional method of viewing homes in person. It's not going to replace home tours, but it will provide a platform to drive efficiency to narrow a buyer's search while allowing an informed homeowner to reach a broader audience more effectively than a classified ad in a local newspaper could.

For those home sellers who want to spend more money, or depending on the listing package you choose with a third party platform, you can have a professional photographer take photos and video; this includes aerial video and photography. DwellOwner offers a professional virtual display while still allowing consumers to save at least 3% of the sales price, on average, in unnecessary commission.

Social media provides more channels through which you can let your friends, family and connections know your home is available for sale by posting a brief message and or photo with a link to your home listing. Facebook, Snapchat, Twitter, Instagram and Youtube are just a few that you can use to help get the word out about your home's listing. In real estate, Facebook is the most popular online network based on active usage. As of the fourth quarter of 2015, there were a total of roughly 1.59 billion monthly active Facebook users, accounting for almost half of internet users worldwide.[2]

Social media also allows you to share information about the community such as your favorite restaurant, neighborhood insights and more. You can provide content that appeals to buyers outside of stats like the number of bathrooms and bedrooms that are in your home. Snapchat is one of the fastest growing social media channels. This **messaging app looks to grow its user base by double digits in 2016, with a larger audience than Twitter or Pinterest, according to a new report from eMarketer. With Snapchat's easy-to-use functionality, a homeowner can easily add video and content. You don't have to be a professional and have expensive high-tech equipment to use social media to promote your home listing. The content you post about your home on Snapchat disappears after ten seconds once it's viewed so users are paying attention. It has one of the highest user engagement rates on social media.

Age Distribution by Social Channel

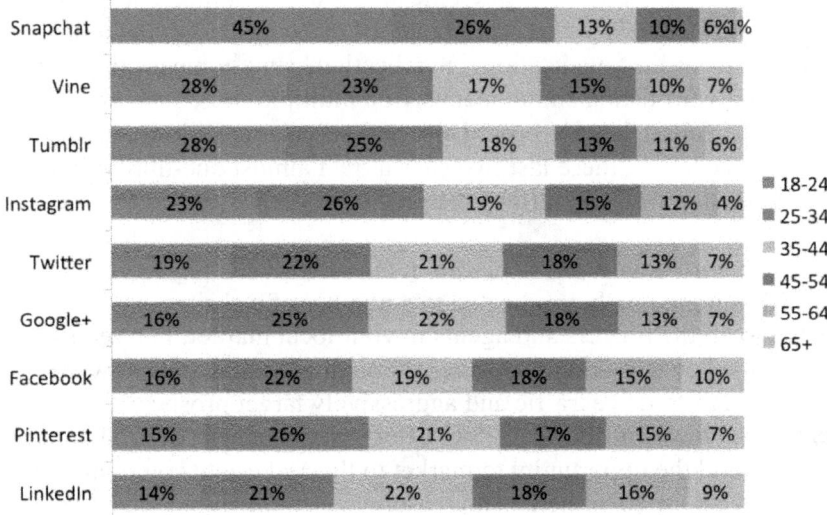

Source: Comscore

So, by this stage you have optimized your photography and created a walk-through video tour, so now you need to write a compelling description that shares information about your home that can't be captured elsewhere. Specifically, you want to talk about the neighborhood attributes, condominium features or other relevant information on schools, playgrounds, bus stops, local coffee shops, dog parks, train stations and etc. You don't need to be a professional editor, but just listing "4BR, 2.5BA in a family-friendly neighborhood" is not that attractive. This part of the online listing optimization is usually overlooked, but is imperative to draw prospective online buyers. If you need some help, take a look at some of the listings out there on luxury sites or sites such as Zillow and Trulia, find what you like, and use some of that language as an example.

Online Syndication

Once your home is ready for prime time and you've optimized its virtual staging, the next step is maximizing your home's exposure to potential buyers through online syndication. "Syndication" simply means the process of publishing your listing simultaneously on multiple sites, such as Realtor.com, Yahoo, HGTV Front Door and, of course, Zillow.com and Trulia.com. Together, these last two sites attract almost one-third of all real-estate related website traffic generated each year.

Fortunately, once your home is placed in the multiple listing service (MLS), it's automatically syndicated to a number of websites and is presented to all the brokers and agents in your local market. For years the MLS held the key to market exposure, although consumers are now aware of public portals to drive traffic and aggressively target prospective homebuyers. However, the MLS does offer you the benefit of broad online syndication and the opportunity to market to the real estate community and target its buyers. In 2016 there is no reason you should avoid the MLS with the number of options that are available for below the inflated commission rates historically pushed by the real estate cartel.

The MLS is the originating source of data entered by licensed real estate agents. There has been a lot of controversy, debate, and discussion over the years as to who owns this data, and who is entitled to access it since this information began being pushed to third-party websites like Zillow, Trulia and Realtor.com. One advantage of Realtor.com is that it's owned by Move Inc., which has a relationship with the National Association of Realtors (NAR) and is thereby able to pull direct data feeds from the MLS to provide real-time, accurate information. NAR governs the relationship across the MLS boards. Sites like Zillow and others have been successfully making a big push over the years to obtain direct data feeds from the MLS to improve their data quality. As I mentioned earlier, the agent and broker community (the largest brokerages and franchises) are trying to move forward with a competing project, Upstream. This project seems to serve their best interest more than the consumer's, as it will allow the participating brokers and franchises to choose (i.e. limit) where they share their listing data. They are late to the party, but the effort is being made to control the listing data and once again try to maintain control of the industry to keep standard practices in place.

So what does all of this mean to you as a private seller? Once your home is in the MLS it will be syndicated to the broader marketplace, providing maximum visibility. If you are using an agent, it's important to be mindful of how your agent and broker are providing "permission" to allow your home to be marketed. It's to your benefit to make sure they are allowing for broad online syndication and not limiting it to select sites in order to protect their commission. Just because you paid a few hundred dollars to have your home placed in the MLS doesn't necessarily mean it will be broadly syndicated and the easiest way to sell a home is by maximizing market exposure to reach the largest pool of prospective buyers. This will also help you sell your home at the highest price with the most favorable terms.

Most Visited Real Estate Sites

Rank	Website	Total visits
1	Zillow	44.19 million
2	Trulia	33.70 million
3	Realtor.com	29.32 million
4	Yahoo Homes	26.48 million

Source: Experian Marketing Services

Targeting Millennials

1. Constantly connected
Millennials are more connected to technology than any other generation, according to research from the White House Council of Economic Advisers. These tech-savvy buyers use their laptops, tablets and smartphones to stay connected in real time to the listings in their desired

area.

Tips:
Create an impressive online listing with content that's tailored to what millennials care about — that's where they're likely to be exposed to the property, so it needs to stand out from the crowd. Consider assets such as proximity to commuter lines, walkability to neighborhood restaurants and shops, and proximity to high-quality schools and parks.

2. Motivated by value
Millennials are a value-conscious group that is becoming savvier about self-directed real estate than their more senior counterparts. They're thinking differently about how they want to work with real estate agents as they take on more of the process themselves.

Millennial shoppers spend more time (approximately 1,200 hours annually) and money (nearly $2,000 annually) online than other generation, according to Forrester Research, and are comfortable banking, paying bills, shopping and booking travel from their devices.

Tips
- Be prepared to deal with Millennials directly, as they are more likely to take on those responsibilities that were historically performed by real estate agents, such as scheduling showings and negotiating the purchase price.

3. Getting visual
This Instagram and Houzz.com-inspired generation are motivated through visual storytelling. They're also big on transparency, so missing information or visuals can be interpreted as a sign that you're hiding problems.

Tips
- Millennials expect to see every square foot of a listing so share plenty of images that leave nothing to the imagination.

- Use 3D technology to provide virtual tours to give buyers a real-life experience when viewing the home on their tablet, desktop or mobile device.
- Be sure your pictures are high quality. The millennial audience is accustomed to stunning home and garden shots and will pass by listings showcasing inferior, low-resolution images.
- Viewers retain 95% of a message when they watch it in a video compared with 10% when reading it in text, so savvy sellers share video content to showcase their property.

4. Focusing on the lifestyle

Millennial buyers care as much about the amenities around their home as the ones within it. Branch beyond square footage and the number of bedrooms in your listing. Sell people on the location and what makes your home different and you'll make a big strides toward selling your property.

Tips
- Mirror urban rental listings by emphasizing facts and images of what's nearby (coffee, shops, restaurants, parks, etc.). This is the type of content that these first-time buyers are used to seeing front and center in rental searches.
- Go to WalkScore.com to get your property's walk score and transit score — those are powerful numbers to demonstrate how desirable the location is for buyers.
- Play up public transit so people can see how easy it is to get to nearby central areas and metros with shops and restaurants.

5. Low-maintenance living

Millennials are generally passionate about building their careers and connecting with friends. Sellers can increase their home's appeal by making it as low-maintenance as possible by being both move-in ready and requiring little ongoing maintenance, even if it requires an upfront investment.

Tips
- Make small tweaks to the yard so it's as self-sustaining as possible.

- Consider planting hearty and low-attention perennials instead of fussy, annual-heavy flower beds.
- Give the home a fresh, modern look to increase its move-in-ready appeal by replacing dated lighting and hardware and installing relatively inexpensive new fixtures such as faucets and shower heads.
- The self-directed model of real estate is meeting millennial shopping preferences —taking on more of the work, expecting flexibility and demanding value —.

Chapter Summary

1. Once your home is in the MLS it is automatically syndicated to a number of websites, although it's important to be mindful of *how* it's being syndicated through the MLS.
2. Take the time to prepare your online property display. Optimize online staging.
3. Use social media to tap into your network and amplify your reach.
4. There is no reason why you can't have the best of both worlds — the MLS and broad online syndication — without paying an inflated commission fee. Using sites like DwellOwner and listing your home on your own will save you a lot money.

6
THE BEST MOUSE TRAP – WHICH MODEL?

There are a number of online real estate models that can assist you with selling your home and saving you thousands of dollars. However, not all are created equal. Stay away from traditional real estate firms if you are looking to save.

I can't emphasize enough how empowered today's home seller is. You have access to new online platforms to place your home in the multiple listing service (MLS), you can tap into broader online syndication, you have greater access to information and the ability to reach buyers directly while saving, at minimum, the traditional sell-side commission (typically 3% of the sales price). The platform you choose to work with will depend on your expectations and the services that are required to sell your home, given your personal situation.

The real estate brokerage industry in the U.S. is highly fragmented, with over 75,000 real estate brokers with only a very small percentage designed for sale by owners. Although, if you Google "FSBO MLS" today, there are a number of platforms that will surface (through paid advertising) that are limited service, flat-fee MLS, and full-service offerings outside of the crowded real estate brokerage space. To be exact, there were 606,000 results generated under that term when I last Googled it, providing an overwhelming amount of choices for home sellers to navigate and pick the best solution for their situation, *and* there is still dated information floating around on the web, along with ineffective business models. There are sites that allow you to post for free or pay a nominal fee (e.g. $99) to post your home on their platform, which is one t that gets very little traffic. Using sites such as this will not sell your home, they are usually designed to upsell you on other programs and features once you sign up.

Fortunately, new money has been entering the real estate brokerage space from venture capital entities and the public markets. Investments in the real estate tech sector increased from $24 million in 2012 to more than $1.5 billion in 2015, in effort to drive efficiency in the marketplace.[1] We are also starting to see other industries entering the market, such as mortgage servicing companies. These industries have invested in this space so that they can move from a distressed asset disposition and crossover to a retail offer in an attempt to gain market share and tap into the more than $60 billion dollars in annual U. S. real estate commissions. (At least $30 billion of this figure represents inflated commission fees taken from families who unknowingly using a traditional real estate agent.)

To Compete or Partner
Choosing to compete or partner with traditional real estate industry is one of the biggest decisions that investors have to make. Should they attempt to drive efficiency and productivity with agents, by partnering to optimize products like transaction management software, customer relationship management (CRM) tools, or other products? Or do they stand up to competition and to challenge the ndustry on cost and service? I witnessed this first-hand while I was working with a company that decided to create an agent offering in order to partner with the industry. The project ultimately pivoted and we launched a model that would co-exist despite being a direct competitor through our national brokerage. I've seen the same challenges at companies working to drive market engagement with their respective product offerings.

Today, these companies aren't gaining widespread market adoption. Although, by being well capitalized and with the right leadership, they have strategic advantages that allow them to potentially capture market share. Zillow, Trulia and others decided to partner with the industry to create a marketplace for agents and consumers to list and search for homes by winning over the consumer. They entice consumers to use their site to search for properties, and assign a value to your home. They gained mindshare with consumers in the industry, so now agents pay the sites a fee to place their photo on a listing, hoping that you will click through and contact them to find out more information. Their business model is primarily centered around the establishment — licensed real estate agents and brokers — to capture revenue for paid advertising in order to gain online leads. Agents simply pay to have their contact information displayed on a properties within certain zip codes and display pages across different devices so consumers will view these homes and then reach out to the agent directly for more information. These agents are not even contracted by the seller however. The information for the actual listing agent is presented in an almost hidden fashion, usually on the very bottom of the page in small font.

Traditional Real Estate Brokerage Model

As traditional real estate brokerages continue to monopolize most markets, saturating markets with thousands of agents who don't necessarily compete on price, real estate commission fees remain elevated for the consumer. A traditional real estate firm's agents are typically independent contractors, meaning they are not salaried employees and are only paid if they sell a home and earn a commission. The owners of these real estate brokerage firms are the brokers, whose primary mandate is to recruit and retain agents in order to drive sales volume to cover expenses and make a profit. In the U.S. a broker will pay an agent 70% of the agent's earned commission on average, leaving the broker with the net difference as their revenue. This revenue is used to fund traditional real estate broker operations, including office leases, insurance, staff, advertising and more. The traditional real estate model is under great pressure and we've seen a lot of consolidation over the years operating on thin profit margins.

Real estate brokers target both new and experienced agents as they constantly try to recruit agents to fill their offices and drive sales. Brokers love to prey on new agents, sending employees to teach at local real estate schools so they can indirectly recruit. Brokers realize that new agents are naïve, so they can pay their new agents a much lower commission initially while charging the traditional 5-7% percent. They also have a chance to convert them to their brand by making them dependent upon it. So agents rely on the broker's services, or at least think they need them, to be successful. Most new agents work part-time and are in their second or third career. They come to the real estate field without any direct industry experience, yet are considered licensed real estate professionals once they pass a multiple choice state exam and easily find a broker to sponsor them to operate under their brand.

Back in 2006, I owned an independent real estate brokerage and was invited to Realogy's corporate headquarters. Realogy is the largest real estate franchise company in the world and is a franchisor of Sotheby's, ERA, Coldwell Banker, Century 21 and Better Homes & Gardens. I drove three hours to the company's former corporate headquarters in Parsippany, NJ to meet with the team from one of their brands, Century 21. I had been solicited by several brands in this same building that wanted to partner with me so that they could enter the market where I conducted business. As soon as I walked into the building I was immediately reminded of all the reasons for which I got out of investment banking. If not for a logo, each brand operated under, it was next to impossible to tell which brand was being sold to prospective franchisees. Each brand team carved out the factors that made them "unique" via several painful PowerPoint presentations, but ultimately, they were all in bed together. Each one operated under the same roof (literally), shared "best practices" with the same strategy: recruit and retain licensed real estate agents. Anyone with a check and basic qualifications could purchase a franchise. No one competed on price (commission) or tried to define their value. (As a side note, at the time of my visit Realogy had recently been bought out by a private equity firm called Apollo, through a highly-leveraged (financed with high levels of debt) transaction. Given my background, I'm almost positive that the analyst on that deal hadn't factored in deteriorating commission rates in their leverage buyout model.) The franchise model itself puts pressure on the brokers to inflate commission rates in order to drive gross commission income with minimum annual royalties fees, upfront conversion costs and to drive growth. Any discussion about reducing commission fees for the consumer did not exist.

Other franchise models such as Keller Williams use profit sharing to attract agents and will develop an intranet site with bait they can be used to appeal to agents. Much of the value proposition of these models is focused on the broker and agent, with limited information about the consumer. In all of the meetings that I had with the different real estate brands, no one mentioned anything about real estate commissions, ever. No one competed on price either. The sad part of these models is that they recruit good, local people to become agents who work primarily with folks that they know and who trust them. Usually it's the family or friends of these new agents who have inflated commission fees — in the range of 5-7% —pushed on them by people they trust to ultimately feed the large regional and franchise corporate systems.

I've attended and spoken at many local and national real estate industry conferences to discuss how real estate agents can generate more business in the current U.S. model using traditional practices. I've discussed and listened to ideas on how to conduct open houses, drive online lead conversion, build a real estate team and more. Most of these conferences do not address how to drive efficiency around the consumer, with one notable exception, *Inman News*, which carves out segments around this topic. Although, with an audience that consists of primarily real estate agents who are concerned about being disintermediated, the discussion is usually drifts back to the current, stale real estate model.

Real estate firms traditionally pride themselves on how many agents they have. A firm will continue to train in such a way to maintain 5 - 7% commission levels. A new agent with zero experience will charge clients the same commission as an experienced agent, regardless of a home's listing price. I've witnessed firsthand how someone from the hospitality industry got their real estate license for a few hundred dollars (the cost of real estate school and an MLS membership), found a brokerage to sponsor them (which is very easy given the intense competitiveness to recruit agents), list a home for a family or friend and earn thousands on one sale. This is typically more money than they would have earned in tips in an entire year and they didn't have to work as hard to earn it either. Overnight agents like this become "experts" and are officially converted to the traditional program. Do you expect this agent to compete on price? Of course not! Deep down inside they know their value is warranted by charging someone 20% or more of their equity on one sale for performing modest tasks

> To summarize, the real estate brokerage industry is broken, inefficient and not pro-consumer. A lot of brands talk about themselves, not the value (commission) they can offer consumers, which is pretty telling.

Over the past few years, nearly 5 million homes have sold annually in the U.S. It's estimated that 1.5 million of these homes are sold by self-direct sellers annually. These home sellers use an alternative, non-traditional model like a flat-fee MLS offering. This segment is expected to continue to surge and is expected to represent at least 80% of all sales in the U.S. within the next 5–7 years — because people are finally realizing that that there's a better, more cost effective way to sell their homes. Using today's volume, 80% this translates to an increase from 1.5 million to 4 million sales, which means $24 billion in consumer savings.

The sad reality is that the traditional real estate sales model continues to dominate and produces a high percentage of sales, driving inflated fees of 5+% on the backs of consumers. Real estate brokers continue to recruit agents to leverage the current system to push commission fees within their network, driving prices higher.

Back in 2006 the Federal Trade Commission (FTC) charged real estate groups with anti-competitive conduct in limiting consumer choice in real estate services. Brokerages were preventing consumers from selecting low-cost providers by limiting services to competing service providers, forcing consumer to go with a high-cost, traditional real estate provider. Ultimately, this was settled with the real estate groups who agreed to drop practices that hampered rival discount brokers from posting home-sale listings on Internet sites.

"Buying or selling a home is one of the biggest financial transactions most consumers will ever make," said Jeffrey Schmidt, Director of the FTC's

Bureau of Competition. "The rules these brokers made drove up costs and reduced choice for consumers, and they violated federal law."

Jeffrey Schmidt
Director of the FTC's Bureau of Competition

Not a lot has changed over the last ten years with regard to most folks using a traditional agent. However, many savvy consumers are now empowering themselves to not be a victim of the traditional real estate model by accessing the wealth of information that was until recently, only available to the real estate industry. Today consumers have several options to help them avoid high commission fees with models such as DwellOwner.

The following section will provide an overview on three for-sale-by-owner/self-direct online models offered to consumers. Some models offer a posting with no access to the MLS while others offer MLS access but services end at that point. Others charge a nominal upfront fee and charge independently for unbundled services. In comparison, models like DwellOwner.com feature a full-service agency offering with MLS, advisory and more for a low, flat fee.

The FSBO Self-Direct Models

Historically, For Sale by Owner (FSBO) models have offered a limited selection of tools to home sellers, and many looked the same. A number of these platforms are still in existence today. There are four categories of options for home sellers to consider. As mentioned earlier, some models offer a "free" listing posted on their site only to try to upsell you after a few weeks of frustration. Others will sell you a service for $395 just to place your home in the MLS, and will then push other unbundled services that a home seller may not necessarily need, such as contract negotiating, pricing and more. There are several schemes that a private seller must navigate. Fortunately, in today's market, there are reputable partners available to assist you through closing under a full-service offering while still helping you save a significant amount of money.

For Sale by Owner Models

1. **FSBO 101 Classified [1 STAR]**

    a. If you want to go back to the 1990s, you can use this tired model which involves placing an advertisement posting on XZY.com, purchasing a flier box and putting out a yard sign. Amazingly, I still see this model being advertised aggressively online and, unfortunately, consumers are using it without realizing how ineffective it is. Home buyers do not shop the same way they did a decade and a half ago.
    b. These websites will try to sell you state contracts and provide you with a list of best practices on writing an advertisement for a local newspaper. I seriously cannot believe these models are still out there!
    c. In actuality, these models are the lipstick on the pig, so to speak. They are used by traditional real estate firms in attempt to make it seem as if they have added a true FSBO to the firms' offerings.
    d. There is no fee for this method, that is, if you don't factor in your carrying cost for not selling your home. The goal is to funnel frustrated sellers back to the traditional sale model.

2. **Flat-Fee MLS Model [2.75 STARS]**

    a. This model is fairly straightforward, XYZ.com will place your home in the MLS and the rest is up to you. You may start out on the same site by posting your home for "free," but ultimately you will need the MLS so this service will push you through the sales funnel to purchase the flat-fee MLS. Prices range based on picture upload, premium placement and other factors.

- b. Ancillary sales include purchasing contracts, yard signs, flier boxes and other items left over from a few decades ago. You will manage all showings and negotiate on your own. No support is offered through the process.
- c. Fees typically range from $99-$895 to get you on the site, depending on listing duration and what's included in the package. The lower tier pricing packages usually charge for adding more photos and charge you fees if you want to make changes to the listing. Expect to spend at least $300 - $400 for a standard, flat-fee MLS offering and more if you want "premium placement" on a third-party website.

3. **À la Carte Model | Unbundled Services [3.25 STAR]**

    - a. Using this model, you'll pay the flat fee upfront and other services will be unbundled, paid for at your discretion throughout the process. I have been seeing new capital flowing into this model, as the sites try to cross-sell ancillary services to buyers through affiliate companies for title, insurance and mortgage — which are all higher margin businesses. One company sold for $27 million in 2014 with a very limited product offering and a model that had low barriers to entry, meaning a competing offering could easily be stood up overnight in this space.
    - b. Home seller packages typically start around $395, although other unbundled services are sold separately (e.g. $750 for advising). Agent advisors could be a few hundred miles away, in a call center in a foreign country, or working with a sub-par local agent. Despite the lower entry fee, you'll end up paying over $1,000 for basic services, which is still cheaper than a traditional real estate model. Again, in some of these models they are trying to drive conversion to cross-sell you their ancillary services in order to drive profitability.

c. There is nothing new or necessarily innovative about these models. They are just another pricing scheme to try to capture the home seller and then upsell them. Some of these models are even being funded by traditional firms (i.e. Realogy), because they still provide a revenue stream to the low-volume agents that take on individual roles, and thus protect the establishment. The unbundling of services could mean that you pay extra money for a house tour, CMA, attend an event (i.e. inspection), negotiations, etc. The objective is to keep the agent in the center of the transaction. I hope to see many of these services ultimately being replaced with a more effective solution, which looks to be the case (see Chapter 13).

4. **Full-Service Hybrid Agency Model (DwellOwner.com)**
★★★★★

   a. A full-service real estate agency model provides all of the above services with MLS placement, online syndication and comparative market analysis (CMA), in addition to providing a local agent to advise you through the entire selling process. Nothing is unbundled (à la carte) because it's already included in the fee structure at one low price point. This model is a blend of a real estate agency offering with technology that has favorable pricing.
   b. Marketing positioning is provided with professional photos, videos and more.
   c. Listing packages can range from $475-$775 upfront, or you pay $1,575 at closing at DwellOwner.com
   d. Advisors are assigned to the seller. These are local real estate agents typically operating under the same brokerage entity, not a third party, which allows for a consistent unmatched customer experience.

Summary Table
Digital Home Seller Models

	FSBO	Flat-Fee MLS	À La Carte	Hybrid Full Service
Fixed Fee	Yes	Yes	Yes	Yes
MLS	Depends	Yes	Yes	Yes
Broader Services	No	Depends	Yes	Yes
Unbundled Services		No	Yes	All Inclusive
Fee Structure	$99 - $1,200	Broad Range	$395 - $2000	$475 - $1,575
Services Offered				
Pricing Guidance	No	No	Yes (fee)	Included
Advisory Services	No	No	Yes (fee)	Included
Preparing Contract	No	No	Yes (fee)	Included
Showing Services	No	No	Yes (fee)	Included
Professional Photos	No	No	Yes (fee)	Included
Sustainability in Market	Low	Medium	High	High

There is no doubt that real estate commission rates will decrease given the pressure of new market entrants, as has been the case with so many other industries that have been disrupted by technology. Today the home seller has never been in a more favorable position to sell their home effectively while receiving all the traditional services from an agent at a lower price point.

In 2015 the National Association of Realtors issued its "DANGER" report (the Definitive Analysis of Negative Game Changers Emerging in Real Estate). The DANGER report rocked the real estate world with its acknowledgment that consumers were demanding lower commission rates and that brokers and agents are responding with new pricing models that would "*most likely become commonplace in the next five to ten years.*" International buyers are particularly shocked by the high commissions paid in the United States, because the average commission paid to realty agents in places such as the United Kingdom, Australia or Belgium ranges from 1-3%, versus the typical 5-7% in the U.S. market.

The real estate for-sale-by-owner models referenced in this section can ultimately place your home in the MLS, where it will then be syndicated to third-party online real estate websites like Zillow, Trulia and Realtor.com, (which are the three largest based on unique visitors.)

DwellOwner brings professional standards to the FSBO segment while offering full-service support and resources to help your successfully sell your home and in turn save you thousands per transaction. It's concerning to see so many online models that are not offering a full-service online solution, while instead enticing customers with free listings and ultimately pushing consumers through a sales funnel to upsell them on other à la carte services. While this is still a much better model than a traditional offering, (with regard to saving you money) it is not as competitive as a full-service home seller model that includes all services at a nominal, fixed-fee paid upfront.

Chapter Summary
1. Not all FSBO online models are created equal - **caveat emptor!**
2. Be mindful of where your home will be syndicated to ensure that it will have broad market exposure (BME). BME is key!
3. Traditional model practices start at the top and they are starting to feeling to lower commission rates. Sadly, there are still many homeowners who lose thousands of dollars in equity to cover needless, "traditional" real estate fees.

4. The three models that target cost-conscious consumers are FSBO, flat-fee unbundled and full-service hybrid brokerage.
5. Be sure to choose a company that will market your home, not themselves (which is the traditional model).
6. Home buyer online trends support a cost-effective model which makes sense. Who doesn't shop online these days?

7
WORKING WITH LICENSED AGENTS

There are over 2 million hungry agents in the U.S. who could be working for you day and night, by offering a buy-side commission through the MLS. Using a hybrid full service model will syndicate your home to these agents and while saving you from paying a sell-side commission in the process.

Real estate agents can help sell your home on the buy-side, and will bring *you* qualified buyers if they can earn a buy-side commission, which ranges from 2-3%. Over 80% of homes that sell in the MLS are sold with a separate buyer's agent, not the listing agent, (although as noted throughout this book, sell-side agents will still charge a full commission of 5-7% and offer 3% to the buyer's agent).

Traditional real estate agents spend 95% of their time prospecting for leads and the infrastructure in the U.S. steers home buyers to consumers. If you are a buyer searching for a home and have found the exact home you want, you have to be represented by an agent to view that home if it's listed with an agent. If the prospective buyer is not already represented, they usually end up working with an agent to represent you on the buy-side, realizing there is no fee on their end since it is the seller that pays the commission. It's factored into the price indirectly, but that's another discussion. The bottom line is that a real estate agent wants to be compensated and placing your home in the MLS provides a platform to touch all agents.

The commission allocation in the diagram below reflects the distribution of a 6% total commission model that a traditional real estate firm uses. Through alternative models, such as DwellOwner, you can avoid the 3% sell-side commission and will only pay a commission if a third-party buyer agent brings a qualified buyer to your home. This allows you to market your home in the MLS to every local agent in your area, while providing a full buy-side real estate commission. The difference is that as an informed digital home seller you are saving 3% of your sales price!

According to The National Association of Realtors, 92% of all home purchases have an agent represent the buyer, although that's due to the current MLS infrastructure. So, the question is: How do you get agents to work for you on the buy-side? It's simple. Place your home in the MLS and offer a cooperating commission. Yes, you could place a sign in your yard, post your home on a select few websites and make reference to a commission for buy-side agents, but in today's market with the number of new pro-consumer models that are available, there is no reason why you shouldn't have your home listed in the MLS. Some for-sale-by-owners go down the aforementioned path but I strongly advise you to maximize market exposure on day one to effectively sell your home by using a full-service home seller program that offers competitive pricing upfront versus the traditional real estate commissions.

One of the tactics for a "traditional FSBO" is for home sellers to honor one-time showing agreements. That's when an agent will contact a private seller directly and indicate that they have a buyer. In this situation, the seller offers a buy-side commission to accommodate this one showing. Again, this is a traditional approach if your home isn't on the MLS, which, not to beat a dead horse, can limit your market exposure.

NAR's code of ethics duties state that it's an agent's responsibility to offer to show *all* of the available homes that meet the criteria of the buyer. An agent representing a buyer has a duty of loyalty to the client, and needs provide for consideration all properties that meet the client's search parameters, regardless of what real estate company is the listing company. In practice, it's not uncommon for an agent *not* show a home if there isn't a co-broker fee being offered to the buyer agent. Their bias is to run a search in the MLS and have homes that offer a "market" co-broker take priority over any other properties. This is based on real world experience and what is practiced.

The easiest way to have an agent work for you is to simply offer a buyer's agent commission, which is typically 2 -3 %. Hybrid agency such as DwellOwner, allow sellers to place their home in the MLS with no sell-side commission, while offering a nominal buy-side commission to attract buyer's agents to show your home to their clients.

Chapter Summary

1. Place your home in the MLS to have agents work for you. Yes, you could sell outside of the MLS, but by using a hybrid real estate model your home will be both marketed to agents and syndicated across a number of online platforms (home discovery).
2. The average co-broker fee offered to a third-party agent to bring a buyer is 2–3%, depending on your local market.
3. Your objective outside of pricing and optimizing your home's online display is to maximize market exposure to drive demand in order to get the highest price with the most favorable terms.

8
THE ART OF NEGOTIATING OFFERS

It might be hard for some to believe but…negotiation is a natural human interaction and can be a pleasant experience, especially when you are already in a favorable position as an informed digital home seller.

The practice of real estate negotiation sounds intimidating, but it doesn't have to be. When you think about it we all spend time negotiating almost every day, with our spouses, children and even at work. If you take what you've learned from those everyday encounters, add preparation time and minimize your emotions to the greatest extent possible, you'll be ready to negotiate your way to a great outcome. Also, with a full-service agency offering such as DwellOwner, the team will facilitate the negotiation of sale price on your behalf to help get you the best deal with the most favorable terms and price.

Before beginning negotiations with a buyer on price and terms, it's imperative to make sure that the prospective buyer has included a mortgage pre-qualification or pre-approval letter from a bank in their offer package. This validates a buyer's credit worthiness to qualify for bank financing if it's not a cash offer. If it is a cash offer, you'll want to see proof of funds. If your buyer is not making a cash offer, ideally you'll receive a pre-approval letter instead of a pre-qualification one. A pre-approval letter shows that a prospective buyer has formally applied for a loan, provided the relevant documentation and had their credit approved for a mortgage up to a defined amount. A pre-qualification letter can be generated for a buyer over the phone or online and is issued after an initial assessment by a mortgage broker or loan officer.

Pre-Qualification	Getting pre-qualified is the initial step in the mortgage process, and it's generally fairly simple. A borrower supplies a bank or lender with their overall financial picture, including their debt, income and assets. After evaluating this information a lender will provide the amount of a mortgage for which the buyer qualifies.
Pre-Approval	An evaluation of a potential borrower by a lender that determines whether the borrower qualifies for a loan from the lender, or the maximum amount that the lender would be willing to lend. Documentation, credit and other information is verified and processed through underwriting.

A good friend of mine told me about a Harvard professor who ran an exercise where he would team students against each other to negotiate. He would purposely have one of the parties show anger and frustration towards the other party by making unreasonable statements, acting in an unfair manner and interrupting the negotiation. He found that the more anger the parties showed, the more likely it was that the negotiations would end poorly. It was concluded that when anger is involved in the negotiation process, it has a profoundly negative impact on the outcome.

I once had clients list their home during what's known as a buyer's market, when there was adequate inventory and modest demand, so I was expecting that the first offer that the clients received might be substantially below list price. I advised the sellers about this in advance, because in my experience, seller sometimes take it personally when a low offer is submitted, and can be insulted enough to not even want to counter the prospective buyer. Most of the time when a low offer is submitted, the buyer is "testing the waters" to determine the motivation level of the seller. Perhaps the seller is at risk of foreclosure, or maybe for example the seller needs to relocate under tight time constraints? Fortunately, after consultation my team, we were able to coach the sellers through the process and they landed on a mutually agreed upon price.

Some studies on negotiation have focused on strategy and tactics, particularly on the ways in which parties can identify and consider alternatives, use leverage, and execute the choreography of offers and counteroffers. In real estate, a balanced approach is the most successful one, and is equally as important as pricing and terms.

The most successful negotiations begin with preparation. Do a self-assessment on your anticipated acceptable price range and become knowledgeable about current market conditions to manage expectations, as these are things you may or may not need to use for negotiations and timing. The next step is to evaluate the offer, taking into consideration both price and terms. Ultimately, you'll want the highest price with the most favorable terms. Lastly, as you work to come to terms with the buyer, keep everything moving forward and formalize it all to work towards a successful closing.

Preparation

As soon as you seriously begin to think about putting your home on the market, you should begin preparing to negotiate the final outcome. It's a natural process. Your first question will no doubt be: How much can I get for my house? From there will flow a series of questions about how much you can afford to pay for a new home, what the bottom line is for your house sale price, whether or not you can afford to carry two houses for a time, when you want to move, etc.

Typical terms of a house sale include:

- Price
- Closing date
- Inclusions (these can be appliances, grills, patio furniture, rugs, window treatments, light fixtures and other elements that may or may not appear to "go with" the house)
- Closing costs
- Contingencies (mortgage, inspections, etc.)
- Other transaction-related fees

Decide in advance which negotiation points are the most important to you. Would you rather stick with a higher price but be flexible on the timing of when the sale closes, potentially even renting the house back from the new owners for a few weeks to give them time to move? Or maybe you'd rather offer a garage full of garden equipment in lieu of contributing money to the closing costs? Knowing your own priorities prepares you so you can offer things you don't want as much and that might be of greater value to your buyer.

Offer Evaluation

When an offer comes in, price grabs the most attention but an offer is actually a bundle of conditions which, in one way or another, usually affect price. Along with price, an offer to purchase will lay out the deposit, financing, time, contingencies and timing of the final walk-through. Both the seller and buyer typically end up compromising in order to make a home sale a reality. A contract, or an offer to purchase, also includes a description of the property and lists fixtures, appliances and any personal property that might be included in the sale. Last-minute disputes can often revolve around personal property, so pay attention to how these items are defined in the contract.

For example, the curtain rods might be attached to the house but the curtains aren't. However, the buyer might assume you are leaving the curtains along with the rods. Appliances often are another bone of contention. Be sure to spell out which appliances are included in the original property listing. If you aren't planning on leaving a chandelier or other lighting fixtures, be sure to spell this out on the original listing sheet. A great way to remove the temptation for buyers to include it in the offer is to install a new fixture in place of the one you'll be taking with you *before* you list your house.

Once you've thoroughly considered and decided upon your own priorities, you'll be equipped to you enter negotiations and to offer up things that aren't of great value to you but that might be of great importance to your buyer. Doing so in advance can also help develop trust with the buyer as there will be no backpedaling, and this will go a long way toward making negotiations run smoothly.

Finalizing

The buyer or buyer's agent will typically present an offer to a seller in writing. This can be executed by email, online or even in person. The seller has the option of accepting the offer or rejecting it and responding with a counteroffer. Usually the offer or counteroffer will spell out a period of time, 24 hours for example, by which the other party needs to respond.

Again, don't be put off by an initially low price, often called a "lowball offer." Sometimes that's all a buyer can afford, but quite often buyers make an initial low offer to test the waters and see how the seller reacts or how firm they are with their asking price. This is a business transaction. Give yourself time to cool off, but still respond within the timeframe (if it is reasonable) of the offer. If you are not sure why the offer came in as it did, ask the buyer for some context and what comparables were used to arrive at the price.

Frame your counter price in terms of what the market commands rather than what you personally must have. Use recent market data to justify a counter offer and present relevant statistics such as change in the number of homes on the market, recent sales of comparable properties, and the number of homes with pending sales. Knowing your local market also helps you to be realistic regarding price, and understanding your own goals helps you know when and how much you are willing to compromise.

Keep the conversation flowing; don't rush the process. Even if you are countering on the price, respond to each element of the offer to show that there are some parts you accept. Look to see if there are other aspects of the offer that might be important to you, especially if you are willing to accept a lower price in exchange for an early closing date, the ability to rent the house back after closing, an "as is" purchase or any number of other scenarios. Is there something else you can offer the buyer to make the deal work?

Chapter Summary

1. When selling your home it's important to establish upfront your baseline price and what you are willing to offer to move a deal along.
2. Sometimes an unorthodox offering (something of value to the buyer) or counter may get the deal done.
3. Remember, this is business, so disassociate your emotions from the negotiations. If an offer comes in very low, don't take it personally as the buyer may be simply testing your motivation. This is especially true if you are in a buyer's market.

9
NAVIGATING THE CLOSING PROCESS

As technology evolves, it continues to drive ease and efficiency throughout the closing process. By using a full-service hybrid offering, you access the latest technology can offer along with the benefit of professional assistance when needed.

The closing process, which depending which part of the country you reside in is also known as settlement or escrow, is expected to become more automated. Once you have an offer, navigating the process is fairly straightforward: after you have finalized your purchase and sales agreement through inspections, appraisal, title and closing. In this section I outline those key items, from both the buyer and seller perspective, that are commonplace for most purchases of a single-family residence. If you are purchasing a condo or cooperative, you may have bylaws and financials you'll also want to review as part of the process along with approval to buy in the building. Here's a list of the key items to consider when purchasing or selling? a single-family residence.

Primary Steps

1. Offer
2. Acceptance
3. Deposit
4. Contingencies
5. Walk Through
6. Closing

Offer

When an offer is presented, whether you are working with a full-service hybrid seller or are self-managed, you'll ultimately negotiate the best price and terms associated with the purchase and sales agreement. This includes making sure the buyer is pre-qualified. Most contracts and forms that are used throughout the U.S. are standardized and are provided by the local multiple listing services. Outside of price, a contract will typically contain inspection contingencies that can be for things such as radon, termites and structure, or for wells and septic systems if there are public utilities. It is customary for the buyer to pay for the inspection. Other contingencies include a mortgage contingency, which states that the buyer has to secure financing (a commitment letter from the bank) on or before a specific date. Outside of the standard paperwork the buyer will provide to his bank, this commitment is subject to a satisfactory appraisal value at or above the agreed-upon sales price. Typically, the mortgage contingency is around 30 days, although with the recent changes in mortgage disclosure forms (TRID) I have seen this pushed out to 45 days. Other key terms include closing date, items included, clear title and other items.

Acceptance

Once the offer is accepted, the buyer will be required to put down a good faith deposit that is held in escrow until closing. This will be netted against the buyer's final sales price. Both parties will execute the contract and begin working towards closing.

Depending on local market conditions you may have a multiple-offer scenario. The best way to manage this situation would be to have all offers received by a specific time and date. That way you can evaluate all final and best offers and provide everyone with a fair approach for consideration.

Contingencies – Between Contract and Closing

Throughout the transaction, you will need to closely monitor the progress of all contingencies to make certain that all deadlines are met. On the day of closing, the buyer will have a "final walk-through" to make certain that the house is left in "broom clean" condition and has been thoroughly vacated.

I remember hearing of an example where there was a home listed for over $400,000 and during the walk-through the prospective buyers noticed shelving was taken down in the basement. This was maybe a $1,500 item at most. The buyers wanted a credit for the cost to replace it. The seller resisted, so the closing never happened, even after all other contingencies were satisfied. The home was off the market for approximately 45 days. With the real estate agent taking a 5% commission of $20,000, the agent could have just credited the buyers a portion of their fee and still retained a lion's share of the commission income. It is becoming more common to see licensed real estate agents not attend closings because when there is a discrepancy or funds needed the first person folks look to is the agent.

You'll have to make your home readily available for the home inspection and appraisal if interior access to your home is needed. A professional home inspector will assess the condition of the home's HVAC, plumbing and electrical systems. They'll also examine the roof, foundation, attic and basement. The walls, ceilings and floors will be checked for issues, and the integrity of structural components will be verified. A termite inspection is another standard part of the home inspection process. If something significant comes up during the home inspection, which is usually defined in the contract (i.e. over $1,500 to repair) the buyer has a right to exit the contact. In practice, this is when negotiations take place to either have the buyer repair or the seller obtain a credit at closing to cover the cost.

For example, in one particular house, cracks were discovered in the foundation during a home inspection. This was noted in the inspection report, causing the buyer to become concerned. An engineer was brought in to inspect the problem and he recommended that the entire wall be replaced. Given the cost, the sellers simply credited the difference to the buyers at closing, realizing that even if the buyers backed out of the deal they'd have to address it either way through disclosure. Other items I've seen come up include chimney replacement, high radon levels, termite treatment, water damage that caused mold and other items that are all negotiable. One way to mitigate against any uncertainty, if feasible from a cost perspective, is to have a seller order a home inspection prior to putting their home on the market. This may cost anywhere from $300-$500, depending on the size of your home, and you can provide that information upfront to buyers. I once worked on the sale of one home that was over 22,000 square feet and the home inspection cost $4,000 as result of the large size, so prices do vary depending on certain variables. Having a home inspection done prior to listing allows buyers to enter into a contract with confidence and provides the seller with no surprises while giving them time to address any issues that arise in advance.

> Homeowners should strongly consider having an inspection conducted prior to putting their home on the market. That way, qualified buyers will be reassured and the seller can address any issues upfront, and avoid the risk of losing a buyer should any items that surface are not resolved. In practice, a homebuyer will often order their own inspection.

Closing

Closing is when the title is transferred to the buyers i.e. new owners and both parties execute all relevant legal documents. Both parties will pay closing costs, the buyer receives the house keys and you receive payment for the house! From the amount credited to you, the title representative subtracts the funds to pay off the existing mortgage and other transaction costs. Deeds, loan papers, and other documents are prepared, signed and ultimately filed with the local property record office.

Chapter Summary

1. Technology has helped the closing process become more efficient, although for the most part it is still a rigid process.
2. Contract terms and contingencies can be managed from contract acceptance to closing.
3. All items are negotiable.

10
DEMYSTIFYING INDUSTRY MYTHS – CREATED BY REAL ESTATE AGENTS

Traditional real estate agents and the industry cartel are notorious for publishing managed stats and inaccurate statements to steer business to traditional licensed agents and ultimately maintain inflated commission levels.

There are a number of myths that have been circulating in the marketplace. Some of these myths are listed below with accurate responses. Real estate agents continue to be concerned with being replaced with technology and new offerings. Their biggest fear is to be disintermediated - it's what keeps them up at night. They've already seen it across other industries and realize it's inevitable, and that at the minimum their role as a licensed real estate agent will be redefined.

Here are several claims made by agents to serve their own interest, versus reality:

Homes that sell with a real estate agent sell for more money.
False. There have been several independent studies done that show that homeowner sell their home for more, especially when taking into consideration the 5-7% percent commission rate. The 2015 NAR profile of home buyers and sellers actually shows that FSBO homes sold for 98% of asking price and agent-listed homes sold for 97% of asking price.[1] In 2008, Stanford University economics professors B. Douglas Bernheim and Jonathan Meer published the results of their nearly 30-year study of house and condo sales on the university campus.[2] They found that an owner's use

of a broker to sell their property reduced the eventual selling price by 5.9-7.7%, compared with homes sold by the owner directly.

These stats can be meaningless, as a private seller may list their home higher and, as noted before, they are preserving the 5-7% commission.

Agents' commissions are standard.
False. Commissions are not standard and the industry has inflated commissions by standardizing the cooperating real estate fee for buy-side agents. This is the fee that is offered to buyer agents who bring a buyer to another agent's listing, which ranges across the country from 2-3% (the norm is 3%). Therefore, for a listing agent to make "margin," they charge typically between 5-7% commission to sell your home, realizing 90% plus of their properties will sell through the MLS.

The industry is finally starting to feel the pressure of new full-service models offered at lower fees, like DwellOwner and, as mentioned in the introduction of this book, the industry expects "low fee offerings" to be the norm by 2020.

FSBO sellers attract investors and low offers from people who won't pay retail value.
That's not true, in fact once your home is listed with a company such as DwellOwner it's placed in the MLS under a licensed real estate broker so it is technically on the market. Even so, ultimately your home will realize fair market value based on market conditions, regardless of which logo is on your sign or if it's private.

If you pay less, you'll get less service from a "discount broker" or FSBO model.
This is completely false. In today's market, alternative full-service, flat-fee offerings provide home sellers with services from listing to closing. You are never alone and you save thousands in the process.

It will take you longer to sell your home yourself.

False. Whether a home is listed with a licensed real estate agent or private seller using a hybrid model, it will not influence time on market. Other factors like price, condition, market demand, location and other variables will influence average days on market. A qualified buyer doesn't care whether or not a home is listed with an agent. If the home meets their criteria, they will be interested regardless.

Homeowners can't price homes as well as agents can. Pricing is so difficult, only a real estate agent should do it.
In reality, the homeowner is better prepared and more able to price their home than a third-party real estate agent, given the online tools available. All an agent does is a comparative market analysis (CMA) and then he views your home to see what adjustments need to be made. With today's information available online, you can do the same by looking at sold, active and pending transactions to derive a value. You can also use a free alternative valuation model (AVM) to find an automated home value. Homeowners are better prepared now that they have access to a wealth of information to price their home effectively without a traditional real estate agent.

I don't have time or the ability to market a home. Marketing requires specialized skills and access to a closed network of active buyers.
False. An agent doesn't sell your house and over 80% of listings sell through a second-party agent. Typically, an agent will take photos, place it in the MLS, put up a yard sign and lockbox and that's about it, while charging you 5-7% commission. On a $400,000 home that's $20,000-$28,000 taken away for you in exchange for some basic activities, some of which are useless. It's not worth it! You can do more! Once a home is on the MLS it's syndicated to Zillow, Trulia, Realtor.com and other sites. The ads you see in the paper are not effective, as over 94% of homebuyers search online. You can and will do a better job using new platforms such as DwellOwner, your social network and friends. Most real estate agents are reactive, not proactive, in trying to secure qualified buyers.

An agent can help coordinate and prepare a transaction for closing. All those forms are too complicated.
False. The forms used in most markets are standardized, provided by the local MLS and easy to complete if not using an attorney, which is recommended. More importantly, with DwellOwner our advisory services are included in our packages to assist you through contract phase and through closing. You are never alone and our assigned agents work with you throughout the process.

An agent will conduct a professional open house, a broker's open and caravan with their office to drive buyers. (Did someone say 1980s?)
Open houses are for agents to market themselves and recruit clients, not to sell your home. Statistically only about 9% of buyers find their home from an open house (if you want to believe the stats from the NAR). Most buyers find houses online in the middle of the night, when the kids are asleep, comparing one listing site to the next, clicking through slideshows, and scanning every angle of every photo. Websites, virtual tours that provide a 24/7 open house, and virtually furnished floor plans are all used to find houses buyers deem worthy of actually visiting. Qualified buyers simply won't waste time visiting houses they haven't already checked out online. Open houses were more relevant long ago when access to information (i.e. listings) was limited to licensed real estate agents. This is no longer true. We have the Internet now.

As the National Association of Realtors®, reported in 2014, only 9% of buyers found the home they eventually purchased at an open house. That's down from 16% in 2004—and the number of buyers who even visited open houses has dropped accordingly, from 51% in 2004 to 44% last year.

Chapter Summary

1. You can do better on your own than an average agent in selling your home.
2. Tools once reserved for agents are now available to consumers.
3. Informed sellers that do not use a traditional real estate agent can actually earn more from their home.
4. Agents and brokers use managed messaging and stats to support inaccurate statements to influence home sellers to use their services at elevated commission levels.
5. Homeowners have access to a plethora of information and can partner with the right online platform, such as DwellOwner, in order to save thousands in commission.

11
THE TRUTH ABOUT RESIDENTIAL REAL ESTATE – WHAT THE INDUSTRY DOESN'T WANT YOU TO KNOW

The real estate industry has been notorious in trying to block competition and market participants that benefit the consumer. This effort has been primarily
led by National Association of Realtors.

In 2016 there is no reason why a home seller should pay 5-7% commission to sell their home. Over 94% of homeowners search online for properties. The real estate industry is doing everything it can to justify its relevance and, sadly, most homes today still sell using a traditional brokerage at the expense of the consumer. There are already over 1.5 million homeowners that sell annually without a traditional real estate agent.

Back in 2006, CNN published an article referencing the term "the real estate cartel," calling out the unfair business practices and concerns around commission structures. This was around the same time the Consumer Federation of America came out with a similar report called *How the Real Estate Cartel Harms Consumers and How Consumers Can Protect Themselves.*

Drug Cartels   Drug **cartels** *are criminal organizations developed with the primary purpose of promoting and controlling drug trafficking operations for financial gain. The term "cartel" was applied when the largest trafficking organizations reached an*

	agreement to coordinate the production and distribution of cocaine.
United States Real Estate Cartel	*Real estate **cartels** are real estate organizations or companies that influence and control real estate commission levels in local markets for financial gain at the expense of the consumer. Indirectly they coordinate and influence practices in the marketplace, elevating real estate commission levels for their financial gain.*

The common denominators in the above definitions are coordination and financial gain. In the real estate sector, the coordination is having a regional marketplace dominated by large independent brokers and franchisees that are all cut from the same fabric and having a MLS board, structured so that co-broker fees for selling another real estate firm's listing are designed to be transparent and expected, forcing the commission level to remain elevated. For example, if the customary 3% buy-side commission offered in the MLS to a cooperating agent, then the listing agent will typically charge at least the same, pushing levels to 6%. The financial gain is for real estate organization to maximize their profitability at the expense of the consumer versus developing a business model *around* the consumer where they can reach their desired returns. Agents rarely compete on price valuing their services — it's a fixed commission fee across the industry.

Realogy, the company that owns a number of franchise brands and corporate-owned franchises through NRT, (Realogy's corporate owned brands) sends members of its cartel to saturate a regional marketplace, to sell franchises to independent real estate brokers and basically offer the same traditional real estate model with a different logo. This ultimately provides them with a dominant market share in a given region, gives them leverage to "set the standard" as to what is expected from a pricing perspective. When a new price competitor enters the arena, the franchise brands become threatened and may not cooperate with the brokerage. They try to dilute its value proposition using terms like "discount broker" and "limited services." This message comes from the leadership at the parent company (the franchisor) and funnels down to the agents in the trenches dealing directly with the homebuyers and sellers. This is how franchise brands historically establish resistance to the lower-commission entity entering a new region and use their regional market share to dictate expectations among brokers.

Despite media, consumer protection groups and other initiatives, the industry has continued to charge inflated commission levels at the expense of the consumer...until now.

There are still over 2 million real estate agents in the U.S. Approximately two-thirds of homes sell with a traditional brokerage, stripping equity from homeowners. The real estate brokerage industry is a $60 billion industry — that's $60 billion in overpriced fees! I estimate that roughly $30 billion on an annual basis is being stripped away unnecessarily from homeowners on just the sell side alone. This money could be used by families for education, expenses, reinvestment in communities and more, versus being funneled to real estate brokers and agents to pay for archaic infrastructure.

In my local market, New York's Albany Capital Region, there are over 3,400 licensed real estate agents and over 350 real estate brokers that monopolize the market and keep the commission levels elevated. Every time I drive by a real estate sign in someone's yard, I'm assuming they are losing at least 20% equity on their investment by using a traditional real estate agent. These are families raising children in the community, who may have modest savings and are trying to provide a good quality of life for their children. This inflated commission model exists primarily because consumers who are not informed and have been mislead by the industry for decades. At least two-thirds of all homes in the U.S. are listed between 5 and 7%. That's approximately $60 billion in inflated commission fees that will be taken away from families unnecessarily.

Informed homeowners now have a viable choice to sell their home without paying the traditional real estate commission fees of 5-7%. Companies such as DwellOwner can help people save, at minimum, 3%

of the commission.

The National Association of Realtors (NAR), a trade group that represents approximately 1 million licensed real estate agents, does everything in its power to retain the current infrastructure that forces consumers to go through an agent channel. For example, most consumers want access to the MLS, which provides an online shared network of listings allowing all agents to participate and receive compensation if they deliver a buyer through a co-broker fee, typically 2–3%. Some agents will not even show a home if it's not in the MLS and others will do the same if their buy-side offering is not market rate. In other words, if a home seller wants to only offer 1% to a buyer's agent, they would be disregarded, which happens frequently despite violating the agent's code of ethics. Furthermore, NAR earns money from agent dues so they intentionally keep the barriers to entry low in the industry to drive revenue (with agent membership fees) outside of their venture capital activity through Second Century Ventures. The brokers who own the real estate firms have agents as independent contractors and rarely enforce standards and professionalism. It's estimated that 30% or more of agents (out of 2 million) do not have even one sale annually. On average, 5 million homes sell each year.

The average licensed real estate agent earns $40,000, significantly less than the executive team at NAR. The CEO earned $1.6 million in 2014 alone while his executive team and board members all earned a few hundred thousand each, according to their 990 tax forms filed with the IRS. In 2014 they employed 375 people with $195 million in total expenses. Their primary source of revenue, which represents over three-quarters of the total, comes from the member dues of agents so it's in their personal best interest to protect that establishment at the expense of the consumer. NAR's annual revenue is nearly $200 million.

NAR — Salaries, compensation and other employee benefits
($ in millions)

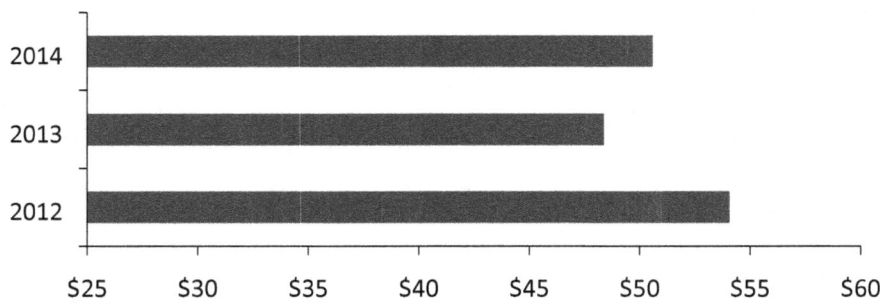

Real estate brokerage leaders are also part of the cartel, especially among some of the largest franchises like Realogy (which, as we mentioned before, owns Sotheby's, Coldwell Banker, Century 21, ERA, BHG, ZipRealty, and Corcoran) that are household names, and force the traditional overpriced, archaic real estate model on consumers by charging inflated commission rates. The United States Department of Justice (DOJ) has a history of enforcing fair competition and rights for consumers against the establishment, most notably against NAR. John Doe agent with XYZ brokerage will charge you 5% to sell your home whether it's worth $200,000 or $800,0000, meaning he could earn $10,000 or $40,000 for the same work on two different homes he has listed. It's outrageous! Imagine if prices didn't come down on travel (e.g. Expedia, Orbitz), stock trading (e.g. Etrade, Ameritrade) or tax preparation. In other industries outside of real estate, market efficiencies drove consumer prices lower while in the real estate broker space, they have remained at a constant level for decades due to internal forces.

While launching DwellOwner in 2016, I also re-launched an online real estate brokerage that was in beta mode. I intentionally tested a market of approximately 3,500 agents with a 100% agent model to allow the real estate agents to keep all of the commission if they paid a fixed monthly fee. I noticed that some of the agents who signed up with the firm actually started to charge lower commission fees without any influence. They realized they could still earn the same amount, if not more, if they didn't have to give up 30-40% of their commission to a traditional real estate brokerage firm. During this market test, one agent asked permission to lower his commission from 6% to 4% in order to get the deal done. The seller didn't want to accept an offer of $270,000 (which was within the first few days of the home being listed) because he wanted to hold out for closer to the his asking price of $275,000 and didn't see the value in the agent's commission since their home was only on the market for two days. The agent made his request after it was made clear that the all of the agents in the group had complete autonomy to charge any commission they wanted. The point of this example is that this agent's mindset was molded around traditional practices, after working with a Realogy franchise brand that never permitted competition on price or value of services. It was almost as if the agent had Stockholm Syndrome. Brokers artificially inflate commission fees in local markets across the country, driving minimum cooperating fees (fee offered to a third-party buyer agents) in the MLS (typically 2-3%) and creating a minimum level of acceptance that most participants support because they are either profiting from it or have no alternative.

> Stockholm Syndrome - Feelings of trust or affection felt in certain cases of kidnapping or hostage taking by a victim toward a captor. In real estate, we identify **Real Estate Agent Stockholm Syndrome** to agents over identifying with the real estate cartel (i.e. NAR, franchises and traditional brokers) pushing high commission levels on consumers.

Through this market test with the 100% model, I solicited a number of agents, which is common practice among brokers. Despite the fact that agents could earn more and charge any commission they wanted, most still remained loyal to the traditional brand under the current cost structure of 5-7% commission fees. The type of agents I attracted were typically investors who just wanted to save the cost of using an agent and could realize the commission themselves when buying a home. Others were strong performers and "got it," while many remained with the traditional mold. In many of my meetings, it was rare that an agent would even ask about the consumer. They were mostly concerned about what was offered to them to earn more, office space, and marketing spend. The agents were well scripted on how they'd compete with lower price offerings, or what they called "discounted services" (value charged) and how they would position that in the marketplace to "win" new business. I heard all of the traditional training in practice, "discounted fees equal discounted services" and more. It was astonishing to learn the mindset of most of the licensed agents in the market with regard to how they perceived the value of their services. After my initial meeting at Realogy's headquarters in 2006 and after actually owning a franchise (I sold the independent company to one of their largest franchisees in 2009), I wasn't surprised.

Back in 2013, Move Inc. managed Realtor.com through their relationship with the National Association of Realtors (NAR). I was working for a company on our marketing budget and planned on allocating a portion of our marketing spend towards the Realtor.com to drive further exposure across our national inventory that consisted of primarily distressed assets. I suspected we'd be one of Move's larger clients, assuming the average broker didn't have the same balance sheet as that of our company, which was well capitalized. For some reason, the person on our marketing team that was working directly with Realtor.com couldn't get a straight answer on our path forward with them in order to formalize our relationship. After several weeks, someone at Realtor.com sent an email claiming their concern was that our online platform could be a potential competitor, much like Zillow and Trulia became over the years. At this company, we never had the intention of standing up a marketplace to compete directly and had to demonstrate that to Realtor.com before everything was approved on their end. Again, we wanted to pay them money to advertise on their site – usually, as the client you are sold on their value proposition (consumer traffic, conversion, etc.) versus pitching to them to take your shareholders' money. They acted purely in their own self-interest and not for the consumer.

Realtor.com Email from 2013

"Good morning. A top-level executive with NAR (National Association of Realtors) just threw a monkey wrench into our proposal. He's on a panel at the upcoming big industry real estate conference and noticed [company name] presence. When I first opened a dialogue with [company name], I warned that competitive issues with some of our members could be a concern. This shouldn't surprise them. The bottom line is, your current consumer campaign remains status quo but the executive team has asked I delay accepting additional advertising for the broker/agent campaign."

Signed,

[Employee] at Realtor.com

The NAR spends millions annually to push their agenda in Washington that may have not been in the best interest of the consumer long-term. They have successfully lobbied Congress to prohibit banks from entering the real estate brokerage business and continue to restrict competition they can't control through their venture capital fund, Second Century Ventures.

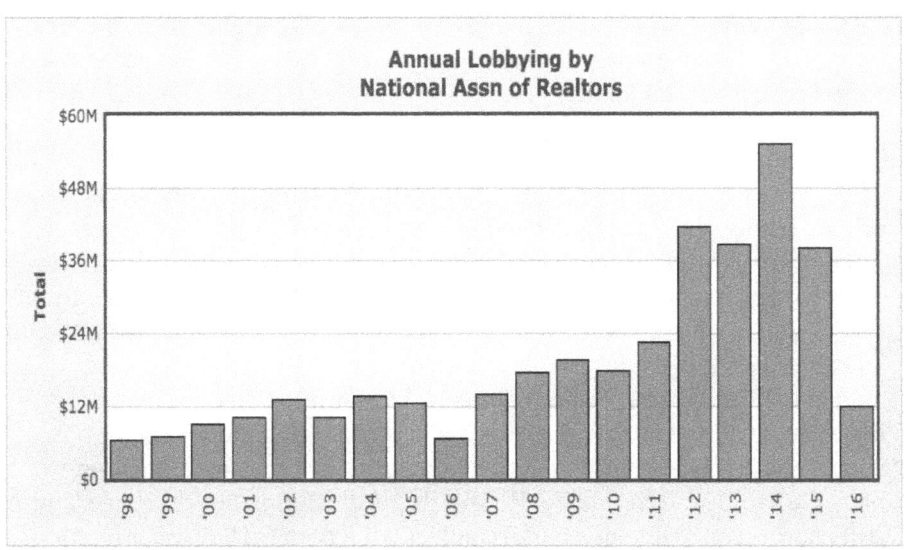

Source: *OpenSecrets.org*

As expected, the National Association of Realtors came out with its own study, which showed agents may help you earn more and sell your home faster. This is not surprising, as they exist to protect the establishment in the U.S. with over 1 million members (licensed real estate agents) who fund their operations, venture capital funds, political activities and legal activities (Department of Justice settlement) to fight off competition.

On NAR's website its mission is defined as: "The core purpose of the National Association of REALTORS® is to *help its members become more profitable and successful.*" In reality, from our research on legal cases with the Department of Justice, consumer advocate groups and recent actions, NAR's mission is to profit from its members and on the backs of consumers through its activities.

> NAR could be a strong industry partner, although it needs to allow "outside" innovative companies and entrepreneurs into the U.S. real estate ecosystem to ultimately benefit the consumer, versus its own personal interest to protect the establishment by influencing higher fees and dated practices. This includes raising the bar for real estate agents' participation and being pro-consumer.

There are even new participants entering the brokerage model, backed by private equity, venture capital and capital from publicly-traded firms. These are all different schemes, but at the end of the day they are driving leads to their market in order to refer them out and monetize at the current cost structure on the backs on consumers. Some are expanding from the mortgage servicing side and others are from the "VC network." One company, Redfin, raised approximately $170 million since inception to penetrate this market and after ten years, it is nothing more than a traditional brokerage with better technology than most firms that don't have the same kind of money. Redfin stopped offering buyer rebates and still charges a percentage commission to sell a home. They are not pro-consumer. They are more concerned about improving margins to plan for a liquidity event to satisfy investors.

Finally, there are the for sale by owner (FSBO) models mentioned in an earlier chapter, but they offer limited support to homeowner with regards to pricing, contracts, and more. Historically, they were very limited and not consumer friendly based on dated methods and techniques from the 1990s. That's one of the reasons I launched DwellOwner —to create the best hybrid, full-service, for sale by owner offering in the market. DwellOwner provides 100% support on every aspect of home selling while building a model around the consumer.

I expect the real estate industry to continue to challenge any new model and believe that ultimately, the consumer will prevail as the industry continues to lose control with online market share! Independent, third-party companies such as Zillow and similar sites have successfully taken market share, allowing new hybrid models to reach consumers directly. They have proven that it's unnecessary to have to go through the archaic "system" to reach buyers. Now, the establishment that includes large regional brokers and franchises is trying to stand up its own online marketplace to control data in effort to take back the consumer. This effort is being made about ten years too late. I talk further about this current project, called Upstream, in Chapter 11.

Chapter Summary

1. The real estate industry continues to challenge consumer-driven models in order to maintain high commission fees in the U.S.
2. Organizations like the National Association of Realtors (NAR) are working against any disruptive model that poses a threat to its interests.
3. There are finally viable avenues for the private seller that offer a full-service offering at a fraction of the cost of using a traditional agent, saving consumers on average 3% of their home's sales price.

4. NAR funded a study that recognized lower-price offerings will be the norm by 2020.
5. Most new technology is being created around the current archaic infrastructure to drive efficiency across dated methods.

12
WHY YOU WILL SUCCEED AS A DIGITAL HOME SELLER

It's an exciting time to be involved in real estate, whether you are a homeowner, entrepreneur, venture capitalist, or industry participant providing ancillary services. In 2016 I expect to continue to see a movement to empower homeowners, challenging the existing industry models and improving efficiency throughout the home buying and selling process.

Today there are already 1.5 million people who successfully sell their home without using a traditional real estate agent, saving billions of dollars in annualized commission fees in the process. There are so many reasons why you will succeed in selling your home while saving yourself thousands of dollars in fees. Below are just a few reasons why there has never been a better time to sell your home without a traditional real estate agent.

Consumer Trends

The market stats are overwhelming across real estate and other verticals, with consumers driving change by reviewing, shopping for and purchasing products on their mobile devices. Consumers want ease and efficiency along with convenience. There is an abundance of information available now that historically had been limited to select participants in a given industry and forced buyers and sellers to use an intermediary like a travel agent, real estate agent, stock broker, CPA or other conduits that took fees. Now consumers can make direct purchases across all of these industries more efficiently and with significant cost savings, all at their convenience, by using an electronic device. See Chapter 2.

Online Exposure

In the old days licensed real estate agents held the keys to market inventory, meaning one had to engage with an agent to even see what was available. This required jumping on your horse (sarcasm!) and going into town to meet with one at a branch office (these still exist). Today that listing inventory data is syndicated out across online sites and shared with brokerages, allowing consumers to shop for a home with ease from their desktop, mobile or tablet device. No need to look through papers or drive around to look for yard signs —all listing data is readily available for home buyers. Furthermore, with access to data, online platforms are tagging, slicing and analyzing information to allow you to search by lifestyle, homes and other factors like commute time that may be more relevant to today's buyer. Once a prospective buyer finds a home in which they are interested, they can tour 3D virtual tours open 24/7 (no need to attend an open house) and view photos along with reviews. By the time a homebuyer contacts an agent they usually have narrowed down which homes that they want to see and know more about the property, community, and other demographic information than the listing agent. See Chapter 5.

Available Hybrid FSBO Offerings

There are a few for-sale-by-owner models available, including the hybrid brokerage model, that offers full service with nominal fees upfront. This is outside of the platforms that unbundle services and charge you more as you move along the selling process. These platforms empower you, the homeowner, to sell your home. They provide everything you need to sell your home and fully support you throughout the process. Historically, FSBO sites offered an online posting, maybe access to the MLS, a yard sign and a link to buy contracts, all for additional fees. See Chapter 6.

Do-it-Yourself (DIY) Tools and Resources

In olden times, before listing your home, an agent would prepare a valuation through a comparative market analysis and provide "advisory" services on the best ways to prepare your home for sale. These days you can determine the value on your home by yourself through several free services using an alternative valuation method (AVM) and also get a CMA through a full-service hybrid offering. Even if you weren't reading this book you could access an abundance of information on what to do and learn about which areas of the home tend to provide the best return on investment. It's out there. See Chapter 3.

The Digital Home Seller Movement

Market awareness is key to driving down commission levels in the U.S. and this starts with the consumer. I want to create a movement to inform people (one reason for writing this book) and help save families across the United States billions of dollars per year. Market awareness is critical and as a result, I created the DwellOwner model and have made it available to every household, not only licensed real estate agents. We also created a podcast, blog and stay engaged with social media in order to provide consumers with tips on best practices to save on selling your home.

The Consumer Will Win

No matter how much the industry resists change, the consumer will always win. Real estate is one of the last industries that has fully felt the impact of technology to drive change across the core infrastructure (consisting of MLS systems and traditional participants). We've already seen technology change the travel industry, tax preparation and retail stock trading. You will influence change and being informed will allow you to save thousands in unnecessary commission expenses.

Next Steps
Congratulations, you now have a higher real estate acumen than 99.9% of the real estate agent population, including most real estate brokers who

continue to operate with a traditional mindset while either resisting or fighting change. You understand online real estate trends and available real estate models and you possess some historical insight on some of the players (the real estate cartel) behind the resistance to change. More importantly, you can sell your home effectively with a hybrid, full-service offering, such as DwellOwner and save thousands in commission expenses. This could be a double-digit benefit on your return on equity.

Realistic Market Expectations

Real estate is local and being aware of your local market climate will help you set realistic expectations. Below are national averages, which show trends, along with a market forecast. Average time on market obviously depends on local market conditions and price, although nationally market averages are currently 30 days for active properties to go into contract. Inventory levels remain low around 2 million active (for sale) single-family properties

Chapter Summary

1. The consumer (home seller) will win and commission fees in the U.S. will continue to trend lower, putting pressure on traditional models with new participants gaining market share.
2. Market information, including listing data (active inventory on the market), is readily available to prospective buyers, allowing them to control and manage a personalized home shopping experience online.
3. Technology will drive efficiency, consumer control and ease when buying and selling a home.
4. To get started, use DwellOwner.

13
THE FUTURE OF ONLINE REAL ESTATE

The consumer will continue to be empowered, putting pricing pressure on commission fees. Many of the traditional real estate agent roles will become automated through artificial intelligence, virtual reality and improved efficient processes that offer end-to-end integrated home buying and selling solutions.

We are already seeing many of the items mentioned above happening in the real estate world. Several new technologies that have been rolled out in other industries are in the early testing stages in the real estate industry and each one has the potential to change the home buying and selling experience. The home seller and buyer will be able to purchase a home with seamless integration across the entire process, from search to closing. Some companies are already attempting to bridge the entire process across one platform. It's still early, although attempts are being made to drive market adoption across the consumer segment.

The real estate industry will definitely change, and will become more efficient and provide better value (in the form of lower fees) to the consumer, although this change has moved slowly due to the forces (e.g. NAR, franchises) that are artificially elevating commission levels in local markets. The market will adapt and I anticipate new entrants will take market share from incumbents while agents' roles are redefined. This will follow with a significant decrease in the agent population, which is currently estimated at around two million in the U.S. Cost savings will be passed on to the consumer, from whom there is currently $60 billion in commission fees extracted on an annual basis in the residential community alone.

Over the past twenty years, stock brokerage fees on executed trades declined by 1-2% to a fixed fee as low as $7 on any size trade with an online platform like TD Ameritrade or eTrade. Imagine buying a few hundred shares of IBM to add to your equity portfolio in the 80s or 90s with a total stock cost of $25,000, only to have to pay a $500 commission fee to your stockbroker on top of that. That same trade would cost you $7, or even be free, today by simply opening up an account. Using that same analogy, imagine paying 7% commission to sell your $500,000 single family residence, or $35,000, when you can go to a hybrid full-service home seller platform for as low as $475.I It really seems ridiculous that homeowners are still paying such high real estate commission fees. Early adopters of online brokerage sites saved thousands and now the mass market is now using online trading. The stock brokerage business still remains very competitive and price-conscious and 15-20% of all retail trades are now done on a mobile device. Mobile is expected to surge as platforms improve and we expect the same in the real estate market.

> We are already seeing pressure on real estate commission, where early adopters are saving thousands, if not tens of thousands, in commission fees on one transaction. The mass market will ultimately move in that direction, subject to market awareness and validation.

The real estate establishment will tell you can't compare a stock purchase to a home, since a home may be one of the most valuable assets you own. This could lead consumers to believe that they are getting better service and value by using a traditional agent, which of course isn't true. I imagine before the masses started online trading there were still a few consumers who used their "trusted" stockbroker to execute trades on their behalf before finally realizing that they can do the same things themselves at a fraction of the cost and have better execution — in real time, with built-in analytics to monitor investment performance.

So what does all this mean at this stage of the book? It should be clear that the industry is changing for the better, providing the consumer with more efficient, value-driven options to buy or sell a home. Furthermore, market dynamics are already in favor of new models to help consumers avoid paying traditional real estate fees.

Early in the book I outlined four areas of concentrated investment and innovation across the real estate retail brokerage market. This is where we saw investment and significant improvement including home discovery and transaction management.

The future of online real estate will merge every element of a transaction successfully and drive massive consumer adoption, comparable to what we saw in the stock brokerage businesses. There are forces that will have to be mitigated, like the MLS system, that lead consumers to licensed agents. An independent, third-party, secondary peer-to-peer exchange will replace it. This is a project I would love to champion to drive efficiency. To date, everyone has been hesitant and delicate around the establishment — and afraid to cause any market friction. No one has come out and said, "Yes, we want to replace the agent or redefine their role to drive ease, efficiency and transparency." Instead, I hear founders and CEOs talk about how they create tools to work with the industry that are "agent friendly." I'm seeing companies that are well funded create agent products that co-exist with direct-to-consumer offerings, not clearly defining their "real" vision or allocating resources to execute effectively to lead change in our sector. At the end of the day, it's all they are not being transparent on their true intent. Behind closed doors many people are trying to crack the code to disrupt the market.

I can recall, in my former life, spending hours with our public relations team, carefully crafting our responses to ensure that we came across as agent friendly in the media. Meanwhile, like a number of other organizations, we were working all the while trying to crack the code and deliver an elegant consumer product that could drive adoption with the potential to disintermediate the establishment.

Artificial Intelligence

So the role of a licensed real estate agent is already being redefined and narrowed, from being the gatekeepers of information to that of a trusted advisor. There was a time when you had to go to a traditional branch office to meet with an agent (as we discussed earlier) to view available homes. Now consumers can do that with their mobile, in real-time and 24/7 to view virtual tours, photos, community information, commuting times and more. There is an opportunity for artificial intelligence to take on a lot of the advisory role of an agent with more consistency and better accuracy with quality information. As a seller you could have an agent that sells one home a year (to a friend of their family) and another that sells 100 per year involved in daily contract negotiations. In today's market the sellers are paying the same commission fee and most likely won't get the best advisory service in comparison. With artificial intelligence (AI) or cognitive computing there is opportunity to replace the agent and be available 24/7. There is broad application and we are already seeing this in a number of industries.

The *Washington Post* recently reported on a professor using AI as a teaching assistant to handle the volume of questions coming from his students. To achieve this, he created Jill Watson, an artificially intelligent bot. The results were excellent. In 2016 *Inman News* performed a test between a robot and a real estate broker to see who could find the best homes for buyers in the Denver area based on the buyers' tastes. The bot picked the best homes for the buyers and the buyers stated that they really couldn't differentiate between the homes the bots picked and the ones chosen by the human brokers. "I guess if computers can beat us at chess and Go (abstract strategy board game), they can beat us at picking houses, too," said one of the buyers. On the buy side, the experiment concluded that the bot can do much of what a broker has historically been good at — finding homes for clients. The bot clearly performed the role of a licensed real estate agent better in this test.

There is a race for AI, with established companies such as Amazon, Apple and IBM continuing to make significant investment in this space.

According to CB Insights, more than 20 private companies working to advance artificial intelligence technologies have been acquired in the last 3 years by corporate giants, including Google, Amazon, Apple, IBM, Yahoo, Facebook, Intel, and, more recently, Salesforce. There have been four major acquisitions already in 2016. Amazon Echo is gaining market traction, with over 3 million sold. Google, with Alexa, will launch Google Home to compete directly with Echo. According to Bank of America, the artificial intelligence market is estimated to grow from $50 billion to $153 billion by 2020 - $83 billion for robots and $70 billion for artificial intelligence-based systems.[1]

> Artificial intelligence has the potential to take on many of the roles of a traditional real estate agent (home discovery, valuation advisory, etc.), forcing better standards across the marketplace with agents and putting pressure on the industry. I forecast a decline in the agent population by at least 30% over the next five years.

AI just starting to enter the real estate sector, so it's easy to envision an informed home seller signing up to list with an alternative, full-service hybrid real estate platform to have his home broadly syndicated with full-service support, while having access to an assistant (AI) that can answer any questions about contracts, online optimization or pricing. Basically, AI will be performing the role of a trusted licensed real estate agent. The amount of data this AI will have, encompassing the entire real estate sector, would be far superior to that of an average agent today who sells a handful of homes per year, if any.

Virtual Reality (VR)

The virtual reality market expected to explode over the next decade, according to Goldman Sachs, suggesting VR will be an $80 billion industry by 2025 ($2.6 billion in real estate), the size of today's desktop PC market. The broad VR application in real estate can allow homebuyers to virtually view homes through home tours and is already being used with new condo developments. VR takes virtual tours to a new level, providing insight on space flow, dimensions and design possibilities. It can even be used to "show" what a home that needs work could look like post-renovation, allowing a prospective buyer to visualize and experience everything. Home shoppers can narrow their search to see which homes deserve an in-person showing. Developers can pre-sell units and provide virtual access to the entire building to preview amenities. This alone won't change the industry, but it can provide another level of depth to the consumer experience and possibly eliminate the need to have to have an agent to view every home. It's still a little early to fully utilize the minimum VR content and equipment available, but we expect that to change over time.

Swedish furniture maker IKEA is using virtual reality as its primary strategy for innovating new products and to manage safety for the future of its customers. VR is used to enable customers try out a variety of home furnishing solutions before buying them. "Democratic Design" is the term used by IKEA to denote this. Home furnishing solutions start from the design concept, eventually leading to manufacturing, and expressing better functionality and sustainability. In 2016 IKEA launched their test app, IKEA VR Experience, that includes a virtual kitchen experience. IKEA technology makes perfect sense and is a great example of yet another broad application that can be used in real estate across the ecosystem.

The ability to layer artificial intelligence over a centralized platform that can integrate every aspect of buying and selling will be a true game changer in the real estate industry. This, combined with enriching the user experience around home discovery with virtual reality and using data based on a user's behavior and needs to recommend homes, will enhance the consumer experience.

Blockchain

A blockchain represents a total shift away from the traditional ways of doing things and in real estate can create better transparency, reduce fraud and accelerate processes to move through closing. Much like the Internet during the 1990s, blockchain is envisioned to enable a wide variety of applications and has the potential to transform a multitude of sectors.

"Blockchain is built on the principles drawn from cryptography and peer-to-peer networking. It allows unique monetary data to be exchanged via a distributed ledger (a record book of all transactions). Blockchain is a technology that allows people who don't know each other to trust a shared record of events. This shared record, or ledger, is distributed to all participants in a network who use their computers to validate transactions and thus removes the need for a trusted third party to intermediate. A copy of the entire blockchain is available to all participants in the network and transactions on the blockchain are time stamped, making it useful for tracking and verifying information." [1]

Blockchain has the potential to reshape the global financial system and I see application for this in the real estate sector. Today more than 42 banks, including Goldman Sachs, Barclays and JPMorgan, are part of the R3 Consortium on ways to use blockchain for money transfers, record keeping and other back-end functions. Bitcoin, a cryptocurrency, was the first application of blockchain. Blockchain can hold, track, transfer and verify any information.

There are a number of ways that blockchain could disrupt the real estate market: by speeding up the system, providing more transparency and offering safer investments to everyone involved. Information in the real estate sector is also "siloed," where we have data on home listings (MLS), property data, title information and client data. All of this data is spread across different companies and databases. With blockchain, this data could all be stored on one secured "database" where everyone has access.

Through efficiency, blockchain has the potential to accelerate the real estate processes. You don't need a trusted third party (i.e. title company) to validate ownership. Closing today can take 30–60 days, on average, with separate tasks done to perform title search (chain of ownership), valuation through third-party appraisal, verification and other closing processes.

> The use of **smart contracts** in real estate can accelerate the real estate process by 80-90% across all participants to drive efficiency in the home buying and selling process.

With blockchain you eliminate the need for verification and identification can be eliminated for a closing. It has been estimated that it could speed up the entire closing process by 85-95%. A buyer's mortgage application and funding could run concurrently with title search and insurance. Escrow could happen in real time with communication across all parties: title, bank, lawyers, appraisers, buyers and sellers, expediting the closing process. The above could happen through a "smart contract."

In Sweden, they are conducting test to put the country's land registry system on blockchain. The Scandinavian country is working with a private company and have already came up with a proof of concept and technical demonstration on how it would work on blockchain. Their plan is to put real estate transactions on blockchain once the buyer and seller agree on a deal and a contract is made. From there all the parties involved in the transactions—the banks, the government, brokers, buyers, and sellers—are able to track the progress of the deal once it is completed. This will drive immediate efficiencies with digital documentation of property transfers with the highest level of security.

I don't expect this technology to happen overnight here in the U.S., but it's inevitable it will happen and change the real estate industry processes by removing inefficiencies from third party intermediaries.

Autonomous Cars
Google has been testing and researching automated cars for years and expects to bring it to commercial use by 2020. Automated driving cars have driven over 1.7 million miles with only 11 fender benders and no injuries driving on open highways, suburbs and cities based on a recent report. There are now other companies including Apple, BMW, Telsa and Mercedes that are developing driverless cars. It's a technology that's already here.

Tesla said drivers have racked up some 130 million miles using Autopilot, which uses radar, cameras, GPS, and ultrasonic sensors to keep a car centered in its lane and maintain a safe distance between other vehicles. Although recently, they did have one death when neither the driver nor autopilot noticed the side of a tractor-trailer when it made a left turn in front of the vehicle.

There are tremendous public benefits to autonomous cars such reduced travel time, lower-density areas and lower car related causalities. In the real estate industry, someone once coined the term "wheel estate," since agents drive prospective home buyers around on weekends to view properties. Some would invest months in doing this and not end up with a sale so best practices were encouraged to gauge a buyer's motivation, qualification and timing in order to determine an agent's best use of time. Now consumers are already identifying their homes online and can use new digital technology to narrow their search before deciding which homes are worthy of an in-person tour. We made reference early to tests that have been done with AI, showing it has performed better than a licensed real estate agent when finding buyers their ideal home.

Autonomous cars illustrate another role of an agent that can be intermediated with technology.

Hybrid Brokerage Models and New Industry Participants

One of the biggest things that can influence change is the introduction and adoption of new models that offer consumer choice, whether buying or selling a home, providing full service at a lower cost. Whether unbundling services (à la carte) or a full service, consumers will have a choice beyond traditional real estate models. At DwellOwner we are committed to continuing to refine our model and make improvements to drive change and savings for consumers.

Another significant factor that can drive online real estate into the future will be having established consumer platforms enter the market, like Home Depot, Facebook, Amazon, Lowes, Google or banks that can automate the entire process, including search, financing, valuation, underwriting and closing. These companies pose a real threat to the industry with their retail reach and could change the competitive landscape overnight. Google has already made investments in the industry that include two online marketplaces and an agent-matching site. They are also pioneering a 3D virtual tour and smartphone technology. Walmart is already licensed as a real estate broker, operating under Walmart Realty in 50 states and conducting commercial real estate activities. If Walmart pivoted to the retail sector (residential brokerage), they could potentially change the competitive landscape overnight with their consumer reach and broader capabilities with $13.7 billion in ecommerce sales in 2015. With regard to banks, entering the retail brokerage space would allow them to vertically integrate and drive efficiency through the processes across home buying and selling. They could sell "pre-certified" homes with financing already in place at approved values based on their valuations and terms for buyers to satisfy underwriting conditions that meet secondary market requirements.

Just over the past few years, large investors, backed by private equity have acquired single family rentals with a buy to rent strategy (B2R). Historically, it was dominated by small investors and partnerships, but with the flow of capital in this space they have invested billions in this asset class. Blackstone, one of the largest and best-managed real estate funds, has acquired around 50,000 houses alone.

Renter-Occupied 1 Unit Properties

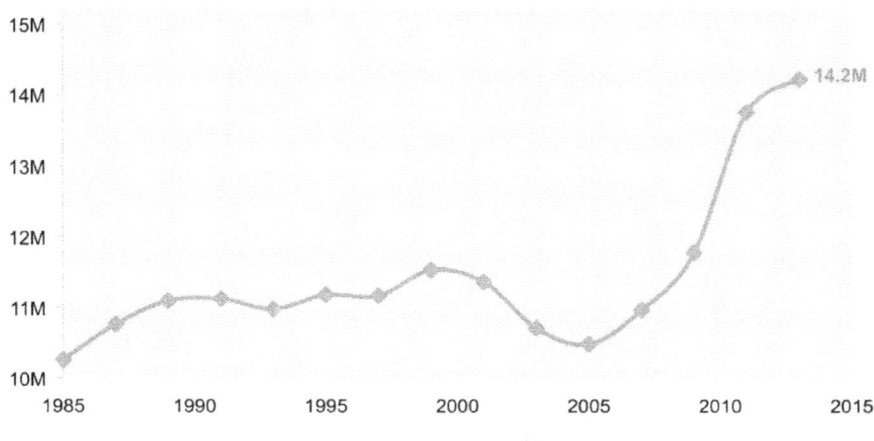
Source: American Housing Survey

This is just one example of how everything could be accelerated to drive efficiency through the buying and selling process. In 2001 regulation was proposed at the Federal Reserve and Treasury that would allow banking conglomerates into real estate brokerage and property management. This effort was blocked. Most recently, in 2009, President Obama signed the Omnibus Appropriations Act that prohibits banks from entering the real estate brokerage and management businesses. If Congress ever changes this law, consolidation would accelerate rapidly. Banks are allowed to conduct brokerage operations with assets (homes) that they own. It's possible. Consider the Financial Services Modernization Act of 1999 that allowed companies working in the financial sector to integrate their operations and invest in each other's businesses and consolidate. This includes businesses such as insurance companies, brokerage firms, investment dealers, and commercial banks. At that time I was working in investment banking for Chase Securities, Inc. (now JPMorgan Chase), and it was an historic moment that was celebrated within the banking community.

Eighty-eight percent of the Fortune 500 companies that existed in 1955 were gone by 2014. My forecast is that over the next five to ten years consolidation, acquisitions and new entrants will significantly change the face of the competitive landscape in the real estate brokerage sector. The constant turnover in the Fortune 500 is a positive sign of innovation that characterizes a vibrant, consumer-oriented market economy, and this turnover in the real estate brokerage space will be influenced by advances in technology. The establishment, otherwise known as the real estate cartel, will feel the pressure and have to adapt; more importantly, the consumer will win.

The New Home Buyer

Millennials are forecasted to fuel the market and are one of the largest subsectors. There are an estimated 80–90 million millennials in the U.S. They are technologically efficient and value-driven, having grown up with electronic devices and spending more time facilitating purchases as a way life online. They will be the early adopters and be more loyal to a superior product offering versus a brand logo in real estate. All consumers today are shopping based on the home (product) they want, not which real estate brand has the inventory.

More than one in three American workers today are millennials (adults aged 18 to 34 in 2015), and this year they surpassed generation X to become the largest share of the American workforce, according to a new Pew Research Center analysis of U.S. Census Bureau data. As we look ahead to the future, it's not hard to see how changes in processes and business models across real estate will be welcomed based on consumer trends already happening in other verticals combined with the segment of the population that will be entering the market.

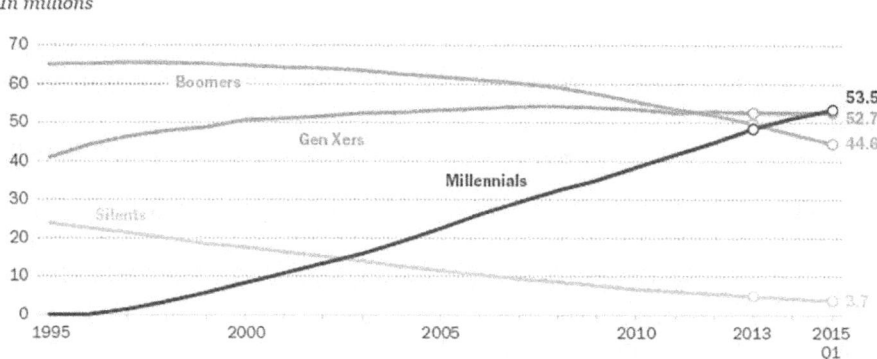

Note: Annual averages plotted 1995-2014. For 2015 the first quarter average of 2015 is shown. Due to data limitations, Silent generation is overestimated from 2008-2015.
Source: Pew Research Center tabulations of monthly 1995-2015 Current Population Surveys, Integrated Public Use Microdata Series (IPUMS)

PEW RESEARCH CENTER

I still consider myself fairly young. My ten-year-old daughter easily taught herself to create a PowerPoint presentation with graphic effects and other animation to present to her class something she enjoys doing, riding horses. This may seem simple but in the corporate world there are still mature adults stumbling to use basic applications. I personally have not prepared a PowerPoint presentation since I left corporate America and still follow the quote from Steve Jobs, founder of Apple Computer.

"People who know what they're talking about don't need PowerPoint."
Steve Jobs

With new technologies influencing change in real estate processes, systems, and business models there has never been a more exciting time to be in our industry, especially if you wish to sell your home without paying traditional real estate fees. I personally look forward to witnessing ongoing innovation while influencing change across all market participants in our sector.

Chapter Summary

1. The market has changed with consumer behavior and will continue to evolve.
2. The role of an agent will be curtailed to a supporting role in real estate transactions.
3. Commission fees will be nominal compared to what they are today, saving consumers billions.
4. Alternative models will continue to evolve, driving efficiency in the market for the consumer.
5. The consumer will win and drive market change.

14
JOIN THE MOVEMENT

I am committed to influencing a national movement to empower home sellers, saving consumers billions in unnecessary commission expenses through archaic real estate brokerage models with traditional real estate agents whose business practices have remained the same for decades.

I am committed to providing best practices, keeping our audience informed and creating a collaborative community to influence change and provide homeowners with significant savings. Here I'll do my best to list a few resources for further reading and engagement with the intent to drive action.

Over the past few years approximately 5 million homes have sold annually in the U.S., with one-third of sales facilitated directly by owners using alternative models. My goal is to have at least 80%, or over 4 million, homes sell without a traditional agent within the next five years. We won't do this alone and need you to be a voice for the informed home seller. Our combined message through our respective networks, media, publications and proven results will drive change, allowing families to retain their equity.

I maintain a website at www.dwellowner.com where you can find additional resources, including case studies and links to further reading. You will also find links to our blog on DwellOwner, as well as video, slides and access to my podcast channel: https://itunes.apple.com/us/podcast/online-real-estate-startups/id1126957995?mt=2

DwellOwner Blog
We created a blog that will continuously feature new content on home staging, valuation and more. You can visit the blog at http://dwellowner.com/blog-list. You can find additional information on some of these topics online.

Eric Eckardt Podcast: Online Real Estate, Startups & Technology
Launched in 2016, this podcast will include interviews with homeowners that successfully sold their homes through an alternative platform, industry leaders and more. You can download it on iTunes using the link below and play it 24/7.
https://itunes.apple.com/us/podcast/online-real-estate-startups/id1126957995?mt=2

Social Channels
Our team is active on social too. Reach out and ask questions and follow our social hashtag, **#digitalhomeseller**! A hashtag (#), is used to index key words and topics on social media channels

Facebook.com/dwellowner

Twitter.com/dwellowner @dwellowner #digitalhomeseller

Instagram.com/dwellowner

SnapChat – Username: dwellowner

AUTHOR BIOGRAPHY

Eric Eckardt is a serial entrepreneur and real estate technologist who has over 20 years of experience in leadership roles within real estate, finance and technology. Eric is the Founder & CEO of Dwellxchange Inc., an innovative capital markets system that connects investors with homeowners, and DwellOwner, a full-service home seller online offering. Prior to these companies, Eric was vice president of online real estate at Altisource. In this role Eckardt was responsible for the growth, market penetration and profitability of Altisource's online real estate businesses. Before joining Altisource in October 2012, Eckardt founded several start-up companies, including a mortgage and real estate company that he sold in 2009 and an online real estate brokerage model that was a finalist for the

Inman Most Innovative Real Estate Startup award in 2012. Prior to 2004, Eckardt worked in investment banking for over eight years in leveraged finance at ABN AMRO Inc., Bank of Tokyo-Mitsubishi and JPMorgan Chase. In his investment banking roles, Eric was involved in over $10 billion in senior bank financings across diverse industry sectors for Fortune 500 and middle market companies.

Eckardt completed executive education programs at Columbia Business School and The Tuck School of Business at Dartmouth and holds a Bachelor of Science in Business Administration, Finance from Pace University. He is a credit trained financial analyst and has been an active licensed real estate broker in New York since 2004.

Eric has been featured in numerous publications and broadcast media, including Bloomberg Businessweek, MarketWatch, Yahoo! News, Inman News, Investor's Business Daily, The Joe Fairless Show, The Washington Post, Business Review, The Albany Business Review, NerdWallet, RISMedia, The MReport, and others.

Linkedin: https://www.linkedin.com/in/ericeckardt
Twitter: https://twitter.com/ericeckardt

ENDNOTES

Introduction

1. National Association of Realtors membership statistics http://www.realtor.org/membership/historic-report and Association of Real Estate License Law Officials (Arello)
2. National Association of Realtors' *"DANGER"* report
3. International Real Estate Review, *International Residential Real Estate Brokerage Fees and Implications for the US Brokerage Industry*

Chapter 1

1. National U.S. real estate brokerage commission rates drawn from REAL Trends

Chapter 2

1. *Real Estate in the Digital Age*, National Association of Realtors
2. Statista, United States: retail e-commerce sales 2013-2019
3. Goldman Sachs; Millenniual report http://www.goldmansachs.com/our-thinking/pages/millennials

Chapter 3

-

Chapter 4

1. REMODELING magazine's 2016 Cost vs. Value Report

Chapter 5

1. Cisco Visual Networking Index: Forecast and Methodology, 2015-2020 Whitepaper
2. Statista, United States

Chapter 6

1. Venture Capital Database CB Insights

Chapter 7

-

Chapter 8

-

Chapter 9

-

Chapter 10

1. 2015 National Association of Realtors Profile of Home Buyers and Sellers
2. 2007 Stanford University, B. Douglas Bernheim and Jonathan Meer -- How Much Value Do Real Estate Brokers Add? A Case Study

Chapter 11

1. The Consumer Federation of America says home buyers pay higher prices because 'cartel' stifles competition. http://money.cnn.com/2006/06/19/real_estate/real_estate_cartel/

2. U.S. Department of Justice https://www.justice.gov/atr/enforcing-

antitrust-laws-real-estate-industry

Chapter 12

-

Chapter 13

1. Bank of America
2. Goldman Sachs

Chapter 14

-

GLOSSARY

Adjustable Rate Mortgage A mortgage whose rate of interest is adjusted periodically to reflect market conditions.

Agile Development Agile development is an alternative to traditional project management where emphasis is placed on empowering people to collaborate and make team decisions in addition to continuous planning, continuous testing and continuous integration.

Amenities Benefits of a property whose existence increases the value or desirability of that property. An amenity can be either tangible, such as a swimming pool or gym, or intangible, such as proximity to a local school or supermarket.

Amortization Amortization is the paying off of debt with a fixed repayment schedule in regular installments over a period of time.

Appraisal Real estate appraisal, property valuation or land valuation is the process of developing an opinion of value for real property (usually market value).

Appraisal Value An appraised value is an evaluation of a property's value based on a given point in time that is performed by a professional appraiser during the mortgage origination process. The appraiser is usually chosen by the lender, but the appraisal is paid for by the borrower.

Artificial Intelligence Also known as AI, artificial intelligence is the theory and development of computer systems able to perform tasks that normally require human

	intelligence, such as visual perception, speech recognition, decision-making, and translation between languages.
Assessed Value / Assessment	An assessed value is the dollar value assigned to a property for purposes of measuring applicable taxes. Assessed valuation is used to determine the value of a residence for tax purposes and takes comparable home sales and inspections into consideration.
Big Data	An extremely large data set that may be analyzed computationally to reveal patterns, trends, and associations, especially relating to human behavior and interactions.
Blockchain	A blockchain is a public ledger of all Bitcoin transactions that have ever been executed. It is constantly growing as 'completed' blocks are added to it with a new set of recordings. The blocks are added to the blockchain in a linear, chronological order.
Carry Cost	The expenses of maintaining a home or property. For example, mortgage payments, property taxes, and the expenses of utilities, repairs and upkeep.
Clear Title	A clear title is a title without any kind of lien or levy from creditors or other parties and poses no question as to legal ownership. For example, an owner of a car with a clear title is the sole undisputed owner, and no other party can make any kind of legal claim to its ownership.
Closing	Closing (also referred to as completion or

settlement) is the final step in executing a real estate transaction. The closing date is set during the negotiation phase and is usually several weeks after the offer is formally accepted. On the closing date the ownership of the property is transferred to the buyer.

Closing Costs Closing costs are fees paid at the closing of a real estate transaction. At the time of closing the title to the property is conveyed to the buyer. Closing costs are incurred by either the buyer or the seller.

Closing Statement A document commonly used in real estate transactions, detailing the fees, commissions, insurance, etc., that must be transacted for a successful transfer of ownership to take place. This document is prepared by a closing agent and is also known as a "settlement sheet."

Co-Borrower Any additional borrower(s) whose name(s) appear on loan documents and whose income and credit history are used to qualify for the loan. Under this arrangement, all parties involved have an obligation to repay the loan. For mortgages, the names of applicable co-borrowers also appear on the property's title.

Cognitive Computing Cognitive computing is the simulation of human thought processes in a computerized model. Cognitive computing involves self-learning systems that use data mining, pattern recognition and natural language processing to mimic the way the human brain works.

Collateral Something pledged as security for repayment of a loan, to be forfeited in the event of a default.

Common Area Assessments	Assessment is the process of identifying, gathering and interpreting information about students' learning. The central purpose of assessment is to provide information on student achievement and progress and set the direction for ongoing teaching and learning.
Comparables / Comps	Comparables (or comps) is a real estate appraisal term referring to properties with characteristics that are similar to a subject property whose value is being sought.
Condominium	A building or complex of buildings containing a number of individually-owned apartments or houses.
Contingency	A contingency clause defines a condition or action that must be met in order for a real estate contract to become binding. A contingency becomes part of a binding sales contract when both parties (i.e., the seller and the buyer) agree to the terms and sign the contract.
Contribution Margin	Contribution margin, or dollar contribution per unit, is the selling price per unit minus the variable cost per unit. "Contribution" represents the portion of sales revenue that is not consumed by variable costs and so contributes to the coverage of fixed costs.

Conventional Mortgage	A conventional mortgage is a loan that is not guaranteed or insured by any government agency. It is typically fixed in its terms and rate.
Creditor	A person or company to whom money is owed.
Credit Report	A credit report is a report detailing a person's financial history, specifically related to their ability to repay borrowed money.
Days on Market	Days on market is the length of time a real estate listing is on the market (for sale). On property listings, "days on market" is abbreviated as DOM.
Debt	Something, typically money, that is owed or due.
Deed	A legal document that is signed and delivered, especially one regarding the ownership of property or legal rights.
Deed in Lieu of Foreclosure	A potential option taken by a mortgagor (a borrower) to avoid foreclosure under which the mortgagor deeds the collateral property (the home) back to the mortgagee (the lender) in exchange for the release of all obligations under the mortgage.
Deed of Trust	In real estate in the United States, a deed of trust or trust deed is a deed wherein legal title in real property is transferred to a trustee, which holds it as security for a loan (debt) between a borrower and lender. The equitable title remains with the borrower.

Digital Home Seller	A savvy consumer that uses the latest technology and alternative real estate brokerage solutions to sell their home efficiency while saving thousands in commission expense.
Earnest Money	Earnest money is a deposit made to a seller showing the buyer's good faith in a transaction. Often used in real estate transactions, earnest money allows the buyer additional time when seeking financing. Earnest money is typically held jointly by the seller and buyer in a trust or escrow account.
Efficiency Ratio (Marketing)	
Fair Market Value	A selling price for an item to which a buyer and seller can agree.
Fee Simple	The greatest possible estate in land, wherein the owner has the right to use it, exclusively possess it, commit waste upon it, dispose of it by deed or will, and take its fruits. A fee simple represents absolute ownership of land, and therefore the owner may do whatever he or she chooses with the land. If an owner of a fee simple dies intestate, the land will descend to the heirs.
FHA	The Federal Housing Administration (FHA) is a United States government agency created as part of the National Housing Act of 1934. It sets standards

	for construction and underwriting and insures loans made by banks and other private lenders for home building.
FHA Mortgage	An FHA loan is a mortgage issued by federally qualified lenders and insured by the Federal Housing Administration (FHA). FHA loans are designed for low-to-moderate income borrowers who are unable to make a large down payment.
Flat-Fee MLS	Flat-fee MLS refers to the practice in the real estate industry of a seller entering into an "à la carte service agreement" with a real estate broker who accepts a flat fee rather than a percentage of the sale price for the listing side of the transaction.
Flood Insurance	Flood Insurance is a financial instrument that protects real property owners from water damage to the structure and contents of their property.
Foreclosure	The process of taking possession of a mortgaged property as a result of the mortgagor's failure to keep up mortgage payments.
FSBO / Self Direct Seller	A method of selling property without the use of an agent or broker. Generally, the reason that the seller does not use the services of an agent or broker is because they want to avoid paying a hefty commission for the transaction.
Grantee	A person to whom a grant or conveyance is made.
Grantor	A person or institution that makes a grant or conveyance.
IDX	IDX is an umbrella term used to cover policies,

standards, and software pertaining to the display of listing information on websites. Most importantly for agents and brokers, IDX is what enables members of a multiple listing service (MLS) to integrate real estate listings from the MLS database into their own websites.

Innovation Innovation is defined simply as a "new idea, device, or method." However, innovation is often also viewed as the application of better solutions that meet new requirements, unarticulated needs, or existing market needs.

Jumbo Loan A mortgage with a loan amount exceeding the conforming loan limits set by the Office of Federal Housing Enterprise Oversight (OFHEO), and therefore not eligible to be purchased, guaranteed or securitized by Fannie Mae or Freddie Mac.

Lean Software Development Lean software development (LSD) is a translation of lean manufacturing and lean IT principles and practices to the software development domain. Adapted from the Toyota Production System, a pro-lean subculture is emerging from within the Agile community.

Loan-to-Value The loan-to-value (LTV) ratio is a financial term used by lenders to express the ratio of a loan to the value of an asset purchased. The term is commonly used by banks and building societies to represent the ratio of the first mortgage lien as a percentage of the total appraised value of real property.

Lock In A mortgage rate lock in is an agreement between a borrower and a lender that allows the borrower to lock in the interest rate on a mortgage over a specified time period at the prevailing market interest rate.

MLS (Multiple Listing Service) — A multiple listing service (MLS, also multiple listing system or multiple listings service) is a suite of services that enables real estate brokers to establish contractual offers of compensation (among brokers), facilitates cooperation with other broker participants, accumulates and disseminates information to enable appraisals, and is a facility for the orderly correlation and dissemination of listing information to better serve brokers' clients, customers and the public.

Modification — Homeowners facing a major financial hardship that could lead to a foreclosure may work with a lender to get a loan modification — sometimes called a mortgage modification, workout plan or restructuring — which will change the terms of the mortgage loan so the borrower can afford the payments.

Mortgage — The charging of real (or personal) property by a debtor to a creditor as security for a debt (especially one incurred by the purchaser of the property), on the condition that it shall be returned on payment of the debt within a certain period.

Mortgage Broker — An intermediary who brings mortgage borrowers and mortgage lenders together, but does not use their own funds to originate mortgages. A mortgage broker gathers paperwork from a borrower, and passes that paperwork along to a mortgage lender for underwriting and approval.

Mortgagee — The lender in a mortgage, typically a bank.

Mortgage Insurance	Mortgage Insurance (also known as mortgage guarantee and home-loan insurance) is an insurance policy which compensates lenders or investors for losses due to the default of a mortgage loan. Mortgage insurance can be either public or private depending upon the insurer.
Mortgage Servicer	A mortgage servicer is a company to which some borrowers pay their mortgage loan payments and which performs other services in connection with mortgages and mortgage-backed securities.
Mortgagor	The borrower in a mortgage, typically a homeowner.
National Association of Realtors (NAR)	The National Association of Realtors (NAR) is a national organization of real estate brokers, created to promote the real estate profession and foster professional behavior in its members. The association has its own code of ethics to which it requires its members to adhere. The NAR has over one million members nationwide. We view them as being the head of The Real Estate Cartel.
Negative Amortization	Negative amortization is an increase in the principal balance of a loan caused by making payments that fail to cover the interest due. The remaining amount of interest owed is added to the loan's principal, which ultimately causes the borrower to owe more money.
Note	A mortgage note (also known as a real estate lien note or borrower's note) is a promissory note secured by a specified mortgage loan. It is a written promise to repay a specified sum of money

	plus interest at a specified rate and length of time to fulfill the promise.
Offer	An offer is when one party expresses interest to buy or sell an asset from another party. The offering price is often the highest the buyer will pay to purchase an asset, and the lowest that the seller will accept. "Offer" also refers to the act of making an asset available for sale.
Omnibus Appropriations Bill	On March 11, 2009, President Obama signed into law the FY2009 Omnibus Appropriations Act that prohibits banks from entering the real estate brokerage and management businesses.
Online Staging Optimization	Preparing a home for sale to appeal to the digital home buyer, using mediums to maximize its online display with tools such as 3D virtual tours, professional photography and community insights.
Online Syndication	
Origination Fee	A fee charged by a lender upon entering into a loan agreement to cover the cost of processing the loan.
Owner Financing	When a property buyer finances the purchase directly through the person or entity selling it. This often occurs when the prospective buyer cannot obtain funding through a conventional mortgage lender, or is unwilling to pay the prevailing market interest rates.
Personal Property	Personal property is a type of property which, in its most general definition, can include any asset other

	than real estate. The distinguishing factor between personal property and real estate is that personal property is movable.
PITI	In relation to a mortgage, PITI (pronounced like the word "pity") is an acronym for a mortgage payment that is the sum of monthly principal, interest, taxes, and insurance.
PITI Reserves	PITI reserves means a cash amount that a borrower has after making a down payment and paying all closing costs for the purchase of a home. The principal, interest, taxes, and insurance (PITI) reserves must equal the amount that the borrower would have to pay for PITI for a predefined number of months.
Point	A point is a fee equal to 1% of the loan amount. A 30-year, $150,000 mortgage might have a rate of 7% but come with a charge of 1 point, or $1,500. A lender can charge 1 or more points. There are two kinds of points: discount points and origination points.
Pre-Approved	An evaluation of a potential borrower by a lender that determines whether the borrower qualifies for a loan from the lender, or the maximum amount that the lender would be willing to lend.
Predictive Analytics	Predictive analytics is the branch of advanced analytics which is used to make predictions about unknown future events. Predictive analytics uses many techniques from data mining, statistics, modeling, machine learning, and artificial intelligence to analyze current data to make predictions about the future.

Prepayment

A prepayment is the satisfaction of a debt or installment payment before its official due date. A prepayment can be for the entire balance or for any upcoming payment that is paid in advance of the date for which the borrower is contractually obligated to pay it.

Prepayment Penalty

A prepayment penalty, also known as a "prepay" in the industry, is an agreement between a borrower and a bank or mortgage lender that regulates what the borrower is allowed to pay off and when. Most mortgage lenders allow borrowers to pay off up to 20% of the loan balance each year.

Pre-Qualification

Getting pre-qualified is the initial step in the mortgage process, and it's generally fairly simple. You supply a bank or lender with your overall financial picture, including your debt, income and assets. After evaluating this information, a lender can give you an idea of the mortgage amount for which you qualify.

Prime Rate

The lowest rate of interest at which money may be borrowed commercially.

Principal

Mortgage principal refers to the outstanding balance of your mortgage. Mortgage principal is the amount borrowed from the lender, minus the amounts repaid to the lender, and which have been applied to the reduction of principal. As monthly mortgage payments are made, the mortgage principal is reduced.

Promissory Note

A signed document containing a written promise to pay a stated sum to a specified person or the bearer at a specified date or on demand.

Property Tax A property tax (or millage tax) is a levy on property that the owner is required to pay. The tax is levied by the governing authority of the jurisdiction in which the property is located; it may be paid to a national government, a federated state, a county or geographical region, or a municipality.

PUD (Planned Unit Development) A planned unit development (PUD) is a type of building development and also a regulatory process. As a building development, it is a designed grouping of both varied and compatible land uses, such as housing, recreation, commercial centers, and industrial parks, all within one contained development or subdivision.

Purchase Agreement A sales and purchase agreement (SPA) is a legal contract that obligates a buyer to buy and a seller to sell a product or service. SPAs are found in all types of businesses but are most often associated with real estate deals as a way of finalizing the interests of both parties before closing the deal.

Real Estate Cartel Real Estate Cartels are real estate organizations or companies that influence and control real estate commission levels in local markets for financial gain at the expense of the consumer. Indirectly, they coordinate and influence market practices, elevating real estate commission levels for their financial gain.

Real Estate Owned (REO) Real estate owned or REO is a term used in the United States to describe a class of property owned

	by a lender—typically a bank, government agency, or government loan insurer—after an unsuccessful sale at a foreclosure auction.
Real Estate Transaction Standard (RETS)	Real Estate Transaction Standard is a framework used in Canada & the United States by the real estate industry to facilitate the exchange of data. RETS was launched in 1999 by the National Association of Realtors and related groups.
Qualifying ratios	Qualification ratio of debt to income and housing expense to income that is used by mortgage lenders to determine a borrower's credit worthiness for certain loan amounts.
Scrum	Scrum is an agile software development model based on multiple small teams working in an intensive and interdependent manner. The term is named for the scrum (or scrummage) formation in rugby, which is used to restart the game after an event that causes play to stop.
Single Family Residence (SFR)	A single family detached home, also called a single detached dwelling, single family residence (SFR) or separate house is a free-standing residential building. It is defined in opposition to a multi-family residential dwelling.
Smart Contracts	Smart contracts are computer protocols that facilitate, verify, or enforce the negotiation or performance of a contact, or that make a contractual clause unnecessary. Smart contracts usually also have a user interface and often emulate the logic of contractual clauses.

	Proponents of smart contracts claim that many kinds of contractual clauses may thus be made partially or fully self-executing, self-enforcing, or both. Smart contracts aim to provide security superior to traditional contract law and to reduce other transaction costs associated with contracting.
Stockholm Syndrome	Feelings of trust or affection felt in certain cases of kidnapping or hostage taking by a victim toward a captor. In real estate, we identify **Real Estate Agent Stockholm Syndrome** to agents over identifying with the real estate cartel (i.e. NAR, franchises and brokers) maintaining high commission levels.
Survey	To examine and record the area and features of (an area of land) so as to construct a map, plan, or description.
Tenancy in Common	A shared tenancy in which each holder has a distinct, separately transferable interest.
Term	A fixed or limited period. For example, the term on a mortgage is its duration, as in a 15 or 30-year mortgage.
Title	In property law, a title is a bundle of rights in a piece of property in which a party may own either a legal interest or equitable interest. The rights in the bundle may be separated and held by different parties. It may also refer to a formal document, such as a deed, that serves as evidence of ownership.
Title Insurance	Title insurance is principally a product developed and sold in the United States as a result of an

	alleged comparative deficiency of land records in that country. It is meant to protect an owner's or a lender's financial interest in real property against loss due to title defects, liens or other matters.
Transfer Tax	Real estate transfer tax is a tax that may be imposed by states, counties, or municipalities on the privilege of transferring real property within the jurisdiction.
Trustee	An individual person or member of a board given control or powers of administration of property in trust with a legal obligation to administer it solely for the purposes specified.
Unique Visitors	Unique visitors refers to the number of distinct individuals requesting pages from the website during a given period, regardless of how often they visit. This refers to the number of times a site is visited, no matter how many visitors make up those visits.
VA Mortgage	A VA loan is a mortgage loan in the United States guaranteed by the U.S. Department of Veterans Affairs (VA). The loan may be issued by qualified lenders. The VA loan was designed to offer long-term financing to eligible American veterans or their surviving spouses (provided they do not remarry).

UNCONDITIONAL WITHDRAWAL

If your home is listed with a traditional agent, you may be able to use the standard withdrawal form below to have it released in order to save thousands in hard-earned equity. Most local MLS boards provide standardized documents that licensed real estate agents use to withdraw a listing, including withdrawal forms which may be conditional or unconditional.

You want to request an unconditional withdrawal form, which means it's a clean release. A conditional withdrawal would have conditions that may include required compensation for expenses accrued or the right to receive commission on any buyers that viewed your home while it was listed and who then returned and purchased your home within a certain timeframe (typically ranges 3 – 6 months).

Once your home is released you can then relist through an alternative platform to avoid paying a listing commission, saving thousands immediately.

Download Form Here – <u>Link to DwellOwner</u> and it's also on the following page for reference.

UNCONDITIONAL WITHDRAWAL FORM

Supplemental agreement to listing dated _____ of property at

_____ MLS No.

_____

TO: MEMBERS OF THE MULTIPLE LISTING SERVICE:

It is hereby mutually agreed that the above referenced Multiple Listing Service Agreement is cancelled, null and void as of the date of this agreement. The Multiple Listing Service member and the owner request the property be withdrawn unconditionally from the Multiple Listing Service.

The unconditional withdrawal shall become effective upon proper execution of this agreement.

Owner hereby acknowledges receipt of a copy of above unconditional withdrawal form.

_____	_____
Owner	Owner

Approved and consented to this _____ **day of** _____ **by Listing Broker.**

_____
Listing Broker

Copyrighted Material

RESOURCES

Home Inspections
All National Association of Home Inspectors (NAHI) members are highly trained and well qualified with experience in all phases of home inspection. NAHI members meet high standards of excellence and follow comprehensive inspection guidelines that are stated in the NAHI Standards of Practice & Code of Ethics. Every NAHI applicant's credentials are reviewed to ascertain that members have training and experience to conduct the highest quality professional home inspection.

http://www.nahi.org/

Home Appraisers
http://www.appraisersassociation.org/
http://www.appraisers.org/

DwellOwner Blog
We created a blog that will continuously feature new content on home staging, valuation and more. You can visit the blog at http://dwellowner.com/blog-list. You can find additional information on some of these topics online.

Eric Eckardt Podcast: Online Real Estate, Startups & Technology
Launched in 2016, this podcast will include interviews with homeowners that successfully sold their homes through an alternative platform, industry leaders and more. You can download it on iTunes using the link below and play it 24/7.
https://itunes.apple.com/us/podcast/online-real-estate-startups/id1126957995?mt=2

www.ingramcontent.com/pod-product-compliance
Lightning Source LLC
Chambersburg PA
CBHW070811100426
42742CB00012B/2327